W9-CNB-977

ACKNOWLEDGEMENTS:

A book is never just the work of one person and this book is certainly no exception. My loving spouse Muriel has put up with me being focused on getting this done and has been very supportive along the way. My business partner Sharon Bloodworth helped pick up a lot of items so I could focus on this effort and helped with some editing. The editors were very patient and helpful as the book came to the finish line. Also the entire White Oaks team including Micki Larson, Alex Duty, Cyndi Castle, Nick Chimerakis, Rory Corrigan, Tom Roffers and Meryl Roberts for pulling together and serving our clients well. Without them this book would not be possible.

Also a tip of the hat to Gary Klaben author of "Changing the Conversation" for his *formula* for writing a book he presented at the FPA Retreat in 2014. I had sat down many times to write a book but his thoughts and proposed process shined a bright path on the process to actually get it completed. Also to David Houle, author of "Shift Age", "Entering the Shift Age", "Brand Shift", "The New Health Age" for his guidance, tips and support while this book has been developed.

THE FOUR
HORSEMEN
OF THE
INVESTOR'S
APOCALYPSE

THE FOUR EVILS THAT WILL
CRUSH YOUR PORTFOLIO,
AND HOW TO FIGHT THEM

ROBERT J. KLOSTERMAN CFP®

ISBN: 1500772674
ISBN 13: 9781500772673
Library of Congress Control Number: 2014914269
CreateSpace Independent Publishing Platform,
North Charleston, South Carolina

TABLE OF CONTENTS

Acknowledgements: iii

Preface vii

Introduction xiii

Chapter 1: Rules of Thumb and Other Urban Myths 1

Chapter 2: Things Are Different Now.................................11

Chapter 3: So What Does Work? 23

Chapter 4: Six Critical Questions for Every Investor..........30

Chapter 5: Asset Allocation Decisions 40

Chapter 6: It's All About Value...56

Chapter 7: The Packaging of Investments 68

Chapter 8: Our Own Worst Enemy 77

Chapter 9: Alternative To What? 83

Chapter 10: Global Disruptions and Dislocations 96

Chapter 11: The Overall Portfolio....................................103

Chapter 12: Manager Selection 112

Chapter 13: Monitoring and Ongoing Assessment............122

Chapter 14: Finding and Vetting Advisors 130

Chapter 15: Conclusion 136

Appendix 139

Part I 141

Part II 144

Part III 149

Appendix 159

PREFACE

The challenge for today's investors is to create strategies that will fight off the "four evils" that prevent them from achieving and, more importantly, preserving wealth over time. These "Four Horsemen of the Investor's Apocalypse" can be fought off and their evil ways mitigated with care, thoughtful processes, and a lot of hard work. The Four Horsemen will be worthy adversaries, however, and the investor must be ever vigilant in countering their forces.

The word *apocalypse* in today's usage is commonly thought of as the end of the world as we know it. The root of the word in Greek is *apocalsis*, and its literal translation is a disclosure of knowledge, a lifting of a veil of revelation. In the fourteenth century, the word began taking on a more religious meaning. Many investors today have a keen sense that there is more to know and some things are kept hidden from them. This book is an attempt to shine a bright light on the key concepts of managing a portfolio in modern times.

The Four Horsemen are the following:

1. Inflation. Investing is really storing capital to use or spend later. If an investment offering promised a return of $776,329 in ten years for an investment of $1 million, few would take someone up on that investment. Yet that is exactly the impact

of an inflation rate of 2.5 percent over a ten-year period. If we can buy fewer goods and services, then we have lost purchasing power. In other words, by simply storing our money and not offsetting inflation we lose the ability to purchase a similar amount of goods and/or services. Less food, automobiles, vacations, and other items we buy to enhance our quality of life. In effect, every investment that does not return at least the inflation rate or more equals a loss. This horseman is ever-present and needs to be a consideration in every investment strategy.

2. Volatility. The up-and-down movement of various investments can seem innocuous when it's viewed over time periods of ten years or more. This is the reason that much of the traditional investment industry touts the long-term investment view: if you wait long enough, you will recover. While this is true, the stark reality for holders of wealth is that they need to use capital at various times during their lives. A withdrawal made during a market drawdown has a huge cost in terms of both immediate capital and long-term potential. Having the tools to mitigate volatility is critical to long-term wealth preservation. For example, a 25 percent market drawdown means you need a 33 percent increase to just break even. With a 50 percent drawdown, an investor needs a 100 percent gain just to get to even! These gains can and will happen if given enough time. Yet, the reality of life sometimes prevents the ability to wait. The new kitchen or bathroom remodel can be put off, but retirees need day-to-day living expenses.

3. Group Think. One source of "group think" (also referred to as the "sea of sameness") is known in the financial services world as the principal–agent relationship. Investopedia defines *principal-agent relationship* as an arrangement in which one entity legally

appoints another to act on its behalf. In a principal-agent relationship, the agent acts on behalf of the principal and should not have a conflict of interest in carrying out the act. For example, when an investor buys shares of an index fund, he is the principal, and the fund manager becomes his agent. As an agent, the index fund manager must manage the fund, which consists of many principals' assets, in a way that will maximize returns for a given level of risk in accordance with the fund's prospectus. All this sounds pretty good on the surface, but a challenge arises when the agent's role of meeting expectations is so broad and the definition of success is so broadly defined that the investor's objectives may possibly not be met. There is a hidden expectation that many equity managers have to be at least in a reasonable range of a relative index. This can lead to closet indexing and miscategorization to meet certain criteria. It is widely acknowledged that 80 percent of managers miss the mark to an appropriate index. A lot of this can be attributed to higher fees and an attempt to be "close" to the benchmark. Whether the benchmark is the same as your goals is a valid question, and one we will explore further. Investors need to carefully consider the advisors they choose to maximize the effectiveness of their investment strategies. One might think that the principal's or client's direction would be the key driver of the investment decision making process, yet the "business" of managing money can get in the way. Is the firm or agent better off with an index-matching performance, or by following the dictates of a particular client? The business of running money (the business of money management) too often focuses on the business of attracting new capital and seeking comparisons on a relative basis. There are tens of thousands of investment options in the financial services marketplace. Unfortunately, the reality is that most are very much the same. All claim to exhibit a superior approach to investing, but as explored in the agent-principal relationship, many are seeking to match a benchmark, while for an investor, that likely is not the greatest need. If most managers are following a paradigm relative to a benchmark, then the "sameness" is accentuated and falls into a commodity-type relationship. Sourcing and evaluating appropriate investment options can seem like a daunting task; however, not doing it can only mean being immersed in the sea of sameness and mediocrity.

4. Global Displacements and Transformations. It is not unusual to think back and reflect on what seemed to be a simpler and easier time to make investment decisions. In the past, things didn't seem to change as fast and an investor could count on certain companies, trends, and themes to last for a longer period of time. Today, enabled by rapidly changing technology and easier and faster ways to communicate, change is happening exponentially. It seems every few weeks government policies and occasionally government leadership change, new inventions and innovations are being introduced. Today we can talk to people anywhere in the world, and no matter where we are and where they are, it can sound like they are next door! The whole notion of time and place has irreversibly changed. This shift has a great impact on the ability to collaborate and distribute information. This ease of communication has had an amazing impact on how political decisions are being made, as it enables groups of individuals to share ideas and draw people to their cause. The unrest in various parts of the world, such as in places like Iraq, Syria, Israel, Gaza, and Egypt, would not have been possible a couple of decades ago. Positive shifts happen as well. It is now easy to see that new innovations in health care will have tremendous impacts on the very nature of our lives. More than

ever before, we can now do more with less. Today, 2 percent of the US population feeds the entire nation and often has surpluses to export. These global shifts will continue, and investors need to be able to recognize and adapt, so their portfolios will shift along in a positive rather than a negative manner.

This book is intended to provide the weapons to fight the four horsemen of the investor's apocalypse by providing insight, perspective, and tools in managing portfolios for serious money needs. If what you want or need is a book to help you "get rich quick" or "double your money" in a year, this is not the book for you. Frankly, my experience as a financial advisor as related in this book won't be able to show you as reader how to do that—not from a lack of personal trying, of course, but by trying and failing miserably. F. Scott Fitzgerald said, "Experience is the name so many people give to their mistakes." I am proud to include myself as one of those people. There is no shortage of "get rich quick" books in the marketplace. If you want to try those books, have fun; lose a lot of capital. This book, focused on high probability methods, will still be here when you're done.

The examples used in this book do not reflect any one individual or situation but are conglomerations of multiple client situations I've worked on in my many years as an advisor that had common characteristics. No actual names, data or personal circumstances are used. Client confidentiality is paramount in our work and is always respected.

Finally, it is important to recognize that investing does not necessarily equate to the stock and bond markets alone. Despite the fact that media coverage focuses almost exclusively on the "market," investing is really about confronting the onslaught of the four horsemen and meeting personal, family, and philanthropic objectives. Investing is serious stuff and requires a serious approach. To meet short- and long-term needs, looking beyond the public markets is critical in designing relevant portfolios in today's world.

INTRODUCTION

I am more concerned about the return of my money than the return on my money.

—Mark Twain

Accumulating wealth on the surface is fairly easy. Over my nearly forty years of working with clients, I've seen that those who spent less than they earned and saved and invested have, with few exceptions, done very well. Yes, there were some who inherited wealth and others who received a windfall of one form or another, but at the end of the day, those who spent less than they earned and invested wisely enjoyed a relatively positive financial outcome. All too familiar are the stories of famous individuals who fell into a windfall and squandered it in short order. Staying wealthy is a challenge for which some are simply not up to the task.

Early in my career, a lady by the name of Doris illustrated this concept for me. I met Doris when I was a representative with IDS in the mid-1970s. Doris was a person of modest means. My role was to educate and counsel individuals on planning for retirement and suggest appropriate investment choices. She worked in downtown Minneapolis in the women's department at a department store called Donaldson's, which has long since disappeared (an example of global displacements and transformations). At age sixty-five, she was nearing retirement. Her compensation was about $400 per month, which was not a great sum, even in the 1970s. I came to find out that she had accumulated over $400,000—a substantial amount of money in the mid-1970s. An equivalent amount in 2014 would be around $1.7 million. Not too shabby!

Of course, I was curious (to say the least)! How did she acquire this significant sum? Inheritance? No. Gifts? Not that either. The lottery didn't yet exist. She had never been married. So I asked her how she did it. She told me that when she graduated high school she wanted to go to college like her brothers, but her parents said that college was not an option because she was a girl. Of course, Doris didn't think that was fair since her two brothers went to college, and in 2014 terms it is totally unacceptable. But she did attribute her accumulated wealth to her father's advice. Her father told her that if she saved and invested the first 10 percent of her income, she would never be broke, and she never was. There are many "Doris" stories; I suspect many more than the minuscule number of "rich and famous" mega-rich examples the media focuses on. Over time I have met more "millionaires next door"[1] wealthy people than any other type of people of wealth. The reason is simply that there are proportionately more of them. Like Doris, they simply worked hard, spent less than they made, and saved and invested reasonably well. They took their money seriously, because they worked hard to get it.

Yes, there are also those who were business owners or who invested in real estate and became wealthy through those means, yet the principle remains the same. They too made the decision to invest, not spend. They were the ones who were living very conservatively and invested in

---

[1] *The Millionaire Next Door, The Surprising Secrets of Americass Wealthy* Thomas Stanley/ Willam Danko (1996)

their enterprises while their friends bought nice cars, joined the country club, and upgraded to larger homes. Their delayed gratification paid off. Their hard work and discipline got them to a place where they could enjoy financial independence and help others in significant ways. Yes, there are those who come by wealth via inheritance, etc., but they are relatively few in number. Besides, the happiest people, in my experience, are those who came by their financial success the old-fashioned way: through hard work and delayed gratification, the best way to achieve the hopes and dreams we all have.

As people reach their targets, their attitudes often shift from "How do I build wealth (that is, 'make my pile bigger')?" to "How do I keep what I have and maintain my lifestyle?" The marginal enjoyment of adding to their net worth becomes less important than keeping what they have.

There is an abundance of information on investing, from how to select stocks to how to buy and flip houses. As I mentioned earlier, this book isn't for the people who are attracted to the "get rich quick" schemes. This book is for those of you who have done the hard part: you saved and invested your way to financial security. Your biggest concern is no longer how to make the pile bigger, but rather how to preserve the wealth you have. You might be wondering:

- How can I preserve my standard of living and live the life I have worked so hard for?

- How can I find the right people to help me do this critical job?

- What key things should I be on the lookout for?

While some concepts and principles have stood the test of time, many new investment concepts have been introduced for our attention and potential confusion. Never before has there been so much information available, and, with 24/7 news programming and financial publications, the opportunity to be overwhelmed has never been higher. Of course, the financial services business has many forces trying to gain the attention of the investor. Occasionally, the pejorative term *smoke and mirrors* is used to describe the feeling that potential investors get from all the "information" they are being bombarded with. One of my favorite metaphors is that of "snowflakes in a blizzard." We all learned in school that each snowflake is unique and different from the other. (I've always wondered how they knew that each snowflake was different, but I digress!) Growing up in the upper Midwest, I experienced my fair share of blizzards. One thing was certain: I could not tell one snowflake from another! Furthermore, the more snowflakes I saw, the less I cared that they were in fact (theoretically, at least) unique. All the information that investors are bombarded with on a daily basis are like *snowflakes in a blizzard*. The challenge is to know what to pay attention to and what to ignore.

The need to identify key themes and establish disciplined processes has never been higher. Old "rules of thumb" need to be reexamined. Previously held beliefs may or may not be applicable in today's world.

Some of us on the professional side of the money business refer to much of the financial information available in the public domain as "financial pornography." It's designed to attract attention, entice, or give a false sense of hope with no real tangible outcome of a productive nature. In this book, we will focus on serious money that is needed for serious outcomes. The goal is to remove the smoke and identify the mirrors to fight the Four Horsemen that inhibit investors' success so readers can identify solid strategies and make financial decisions with confidence.

CHAPTER 1

RULES OF THUMB AND OTHER URBAN MYTHS

Fables should be taught as fables, myths as myths, and miracles as poetic fantasies. To teach superstitions as truths is a most terrible thing. The child mind accepts and believes them, and only through great pain and perhaps tragedy can he be after years relieved of them.

—Hypatia (Greek/Egyptian philosopher)

Given a choice between a hard way to do things and an easy way, most of us will take the easy way. On the other hand, if you are in the high net worth segment of the population (for whom this book is written), you also know that sometimes the "shortcut" or "easy" answer has hidden costs and consequences. After all, you most likely didn't get to your current status by taking shortcuts. We commonly use the term "Rules of Thumb" to describe these shortcuts.

The financial world is filled with a number of "rules of thumb". Some may have some bearing on the proper construction of a portfolio, some may have less, and some are just simply and hopelessly out of date. When fighting off the forces of the Four Horsemen, we shouldn't expend any energy or time on old sayings that lead us in the wrong direction. Let's take a look at some of the more common ones, see what they are based on, and what cautions one should employ in the construction of a portfolio designed to meet both short- and long-term needs.

Rule of Thumb: 100 — Your Age = Percentage in Stocks

For example, if someone is age sixty-five currently, that would suggest that only 35 percent of his or her portfolio would be allocated to stocks. Not a week goes by that I (or a member of my firm's team) don't hear that "rule" used in a statement or question. This old saying has been around for many decades, and decades ago it was fairly useful.

The First Horseman Clues

The "100 – Age" rule for the percentage invested in stocks ignores the impact of inflation over time and leaves you exposed with no protection against the first horseman, inflation. It worked fine when retirement was expected to last only a few years. Today, retirement is often counted in decades, not years.

It may be helpful here to acknowledge where the whole idea of retirement came from. Retirement is actually a fairly new concept; for most of humanity's history, the notion of retirement did not even exist. The idea of retirement started in the 1880s when the then chancellor of Germany, Otto Von Bismarck, instituted a social program for those over the age of sixty-five. His reasoning was quite simple: the average life expectancy for a male was forty-seven at the time, and if someone had beaten the odds and lived eighteen years beyond his life expectancy, then there should be some support for that person. That's where age sixty-five as a retirement age got its beginning! Obviously, life expectancies have increased dramatically since that time.

One of the problems of the US Social Security system is that increased life expectancy has not been recognized in the system. It is common knowledge that adjusting the retirement age by adding as few as five to seven years would put the system on sound footing. How does this affect portfolios designed for long-term security? The big issue today is the ability to offset inflation. Those of us in the "boomer" generation remember grandparents retiring at age sixty-two to sixty-five, living for five to ten years, and then leaving us. For most people of that time, planning for retirement was planning for a fairly short period of time. Inflation over a short period of time is important, but its significance increases dramatically with time.

For example, if you retire and have a need for $100,000 per year in retirement, seven years later the need, adjusted for inflation, is $122,987, using 3 percent as the number for the consumer price index (CPI). In the 1950s, the "100 – age in stocks" rule probably worked okay. Let's bring that into current focus. If a person lives for twenty years, then his new need is now $180,611, a huge difference that will require more capital to solve this new-world dynamic. The horseman representing inflation is very real and the Age-100 "rule of thumb" ignores the impact of inflation on the ability to design an effective portfolio. Effective strategies need to reflect current realities and not honor an old and out-of-date paradigm.

It is especially daunting to consider is all the new medical technology and innovation. Our life expectancies are continuing to expand, and technologies are being developed every day to push them out further than we ever would have believed possible. The biggest unknown is that we truly have little understanding of how this will affect our lives. What we do know is that fixed-income investments like bonds have little power

Second Horseman Clues

The second horseman, volatility, can have a huge impact on the viability of the 4 percent rule. If you start making withdrawals during a significant bear market, common sense would indicate that the lesser amount of capital left available to work will be a significant drag. For that reason, having adequate cash reserves of twelve to eighteen months will help mitigate the damage.

to offset inflation over long periods of time, and that proper techniques and strategy design for portfolios that can provide the flexibility for dealing with these unknowns is critical to financial success.

Rule of Thumb: The 4 Percent Rule

During my career, it's been a joy to watch the vast majority of our clients support their lifestyle in retirement with their portfolios. But not every story is a happy one. Frank and Sally entered retirement with a significant sum of capital and enjoyed the good life for many years. Frank owned a business "that almost ran itself" and had a second home with all the toys that went with it. Frank and Sally were very risk adverse and invested entirely in bank CDs and bond funds. It worked for a long time, but the cost of everything kept going up and the size of their portfolio shrank with each withdrawal. Eventually the business's key employee decided it was time to move on. This was not an expected event. The assets of the business were sold at auction. The second home had to be sold, as well as all the toys. Looking back, Frank wishes he had been a little more focused on the long term and more realistic about the business. Their portfolio design could not keep up with their needs.

Tom and Janet also worked hard and decided to retire with $3 million of capital. They felt they were rich and made all kinds of "one time" purchases. Unfortunately, their serial one-time purchases ate into their capital. They decided to buy a piece of land and develop it for people wanting second homes. They hoped this would make up the difference and make them "whole" again. Unfortunately, their lack of experience in real estate development showed, and then the Great Recession hit. To make a long story short, their portfolio design could not keep up with their serial one-time events, and their "swing for the fences" investment strategy left them with little more than a lot of disappointments and a need to radically change their lifestyle. Excess withdrawals of capital often lead to less than desirable results.

A considerable amount of research and work has been done on how much can be withdrawn from a portfolio safely. Some of the more notable work has been done by William Bengen,[2] Jonathan Guyton,[3] Michael Kitches,[4] Wade Pfau,[5] among others. Each of them used varied assumptions and came up with different answers based on those assumptions. Each of their papers is referenced in the footnotes and can be accessed for further information, and each brings a different approach to how the distribution should be implemented. In the case of Guyton's work, distributions in some years are adjusted up for inflation, but in years where the equity markets are down, the amount is frozen. Guyton's work also assumes a more broadly diversified portfolio than Bengen's and the option for larger equity exposure leading to higher initial distributions than Bengen's 4 percent rule. All of this work has nuances and insight to add to the process.

---

[2] William Bengen, "Determining Withdrawal Rates using Historical Data," http://www.retailinvestor.org/pdf/Bengen1.pdf

[3] Jonathan Guyton, "Decision Rules and Maximum Initial Withdrawal Rates," http://cornerstonewealthadvisors.com/files/08-06_WebsiteArticle.pdf

[4] Michael Kitches, "Should Equity Exposure Decrease In Retirement, or Is a Rising Equity Glidepath Actually Better?" http://www.kitces.com/blog/should-equity-exposure-decrease-in-retirement-or-is-a-rising-equity-glidepath-actually-better/

[5] Wade Pfau, "Asset Valuations and Safe Portfolio Withdrawal Rates," http://wpfau.blogspot.com/2013/06/asset-valuations-and-safe-portfolio.html

That being said, there are some differences that should be noted for those looking ahead long term. First, the nature of investment returns has changed over the last few decades. For many decades the return characteristics were very different from what the current world offers. For equities it was not uncommon for half of the return to come from dividends. In 2014 with less than 2 percent dividend yields, are these studies still valid?

> ## Fourth Horseman Clues
>
> Environments for investing are constantly in a state of flux. The fourth horseman, global displacements and transformations, will present conflicting data using different time frames. The knowledge we have worked so hard to accumulate may work to our disadvantage. The global changes in business due to instant communication have led to higher correlations in the liquid investment markets.

If, for most of the time, the amount of distribution was the dividend and interest yield and the capital was allowed to grow, does that account for the success of the 4 percent rule? In the current investing environment of 2 to 3 percent interest and less than 2 percent dividends from quality stocks, will equity growth continue to meet the need with 1 to 3 percent gross domestic product (GDP) growth? The 4 percent rule worked in an environment where bonds were 4 to 6 percent and equities were in the 6 to 9 percent range. If inflation stays in the 1 to 2 percent range, the 4 percent rule has a fighting chance. If not, it may create an unrealistic expectation. There may be a need to explore outside the traditional markets to meet longer-term needs.

Rule of Thumb: 80 Percent of Current Income for Retirement Needs

It is commonly assumed that your living expenses will be lower in retirement. It is hard to dispute this on a theoretical basis. For example, the cost to travel to work, work-related clothing, and so forth will be gone. My experience may be skewed, since my firm's clients are higher-income, upper-net worth folks, but my experience is that, especially in the early years, most people's spend doesn't change in retirement; they just spend on different things.

For example, Joe and Peggy retired from executive positions, Joe as an executive VP and Peggy as a president of a small, publicly held technology firm. Both had wisely diversified their options and stock grants over the years and had accumulated a significant portfolio.

They decided to "downsize" to a condo in a prestigious part of the city. Their big home sold for a great price. The condo was half the size of their home (the successful part of the "downsizing"), and it was within $50,000 of the price of the home they sold. Unfortunately, it was $50,000 more! Of course, new furnishings were also needed, as the traditional furniture they currently owned just wouldn't do in the sleek, new, contemporary condo.

Joe and Peggy had a number of things on their "bucket list" that they had been putting off since their careers demanded all their time and attention. Travel, a golf club membership, and spending more time with the children and grandchildren all were part of their new lifestyle and presented needs for income-producing capital. Joe and Peggy's experience demonstrates that while in fact some of our expenses do go away in retirement, new ones will come up. For most of us, life is often much like a game of "whack-a-mole," and as soon as one of life's events gets knocked down, another pops up. This will not change in retirement. New life means new things to work on.

My experience is that you will spend as much in retirement as you spend now, and may have the temptation to spend even more. On the lower end of the income wealth spectrum, the costs that will go away may be more significant and the expectations going forward may not be as high. Other advisors may argue that after a few years, this may moderate as travel may decrease as people age, and to some extent that is possible. That being said, we also know many older people who lead very active lives, and their costs do not go down. The other factor that may present itself is higher health-care costs. All in all, the conservative approach is to plan your needs around your current lifestyle needs. Many people find it difficult and in some cases impossible to lower the level of their lifestyle. Quitting the country club or selling the boat is much harder than most people think. I've seen too many sad stories involving lifestyle expenditures that some consider easy choices yet these expenditures for clubs, homes, travel are an integral part of a person's life and are difficult to eliminate. Often I hear "well I can just cut that expense if things aren't going well". Easy to say, hard to do.

Rule of Thumb: Investment Expenses Are a Drag on Performance

Well, duh! Of course any expense is a drag if it is not appropriate or necessary. If people have the time, skills, interest, and expertise to manage a portfolio, then they absolutely should. They would be silly not to! On the other hand, it is even sillier to buy a poor investment because it appears to be "free." Take the case of Phyllis and Nate. They approached my firm as prospects with a portfolio of $4 million. They had purchased variable annuity products, as they had been told there was "no fee" to purchase. What they didn't know was that the internal expenses of that investment vehicle were more than 3 percent! *And* if they surrendered (sold) the contracts in the first ten years, there was a surrender penalty, just to access their funds. By the way, the underlying investment vehicle was an index. Index? Sounds good so far, right? Aren't index funds cheap? This index did not include dividends. Hmm, another 2 percent cost. Not very cheap, is it?

Still other clients become maniacal in their pursuit of an inexpensive investment solution, ignoring ideas that may make sense. Perhaps because they read an article that said indexing makes sense, they buy a fund with little to no thought as to how it fits into an overall strategy. They believe looking anywhere outside of that "absolute lowest cost" paradigm is silly, so they bypass otherwise good opportunities.

In the end, receiving value for an expenditure not only makes sense, but it is the prime objective in choosing an investment strategy or investment advisor. Like most things in life, the extreme positions at both ends of the spectrum may make passionate points, but the best answer lies somewhere in the middle. You should not only expect but demand to know how and where the value of a particular approach or process comes from. That is only reasonable and fair. Full disclosure should be the rule not the exception.

Things to do and watch for...

Key things to consider in evaluating fees:

- Have you accounted for all levels of expenses?

- Is there a reward (through higher net returns) in the higher-fee alternative?

- Have you been provided the highest level of transparency into fees?

Rule of Thumb: Taxes Drag on Portfolio Performance

Another "well, duh!" is deserved here. Minimizing taxes paid is important and cannot be ignored. At the same time, don't ignore the after-tax returns and their overall impact on a portfolio's ability to deliver financial security.

Alice *hated* taxes. She was in the highest tax bracket and hated taxes so much that she put her entire portfolio in municipal bonds. It worked well for many years as the after-tax yields served her well. However, she did not have any inflation protection, and as interest rates fell, so did her ability to reinvest and get a good return.

Peter also hated taxes. He had a modest income and did not pay any taxes. But his after-tax yield on other investments would have provided more net after-tax income than the municipals provided. He would have enjoyed the higher income, but his tax avoidance at all costs prevented him from seeing the opportunity.

Some might consider taxes as a fifth horseman in the investment apocalypse. Yes, taxes play a role and need to be part of the evaluation process. That being said, the focus needs to be on what's left after taxes, not the amount of tax. If an investor ends up with more net after tax, that is, of course, a good thing. Tax policy is changing constantly, and consequently so are the best after-tax investment opportunities. One should not let taxes be the tail that wags the dog.

CHAPTER 2

THINGS ARE DIFFERENT NOW

In times of rapid change, experience could be your worst enemy.

—*J. Paul Getty*

As has often been said about investing, usually at the extreme high or low of a market, "things are different now." Those words are the most dangerous words in investing. One cannot dispute the notion that we are always in a constant state of flux; in some cases, it is actually a form of progress. In fact our fourth horseman, Global Displacements and Dislocations exposes the risk that rapid change brings. One of the most significant changes in the world of investing has been the access to data that was previously very expensive to obtain, if available at all. Newspapers carried some business news and the three major broadcast networks were often the only choices. In the 1980s CNBC began broadcasting and started to catch the attention of individuals. Since that time other news outlets, such as Fox Business and Bloomberg, have entered the mix, increasing the competition for our attention.

But getting your attention is not the same as providing useful data. Media is wonderful for "the moment." But to be useful, data must be transformed into information and then still into wisdom.

> ## Things to do and watch for...
>
> Things to Consider in Acquiring Research:
>
> • Who benefits if you use this research? You or the firm providing it?
>
> • How will you handle conflicting points of view?
>
> • What is your budget for research?

The currency of media is advertising, and so it should come as no surprise that the host of a financial show's focus is to yell, honk horns, and use flashing lights to make a few salient points. Occasionally, I am asked if I watch any of these shows, and I confess that I seldom do. I used to, but then learned that the likelihood of gaining useful wisdom from these shows is actually quite low. Personally, I prefer to seek data and wisdom from those whose living is not driven by a need to sell advertising, from sources where the prime customer is me, not the advertiser. If the accountability is to the advertiser, I need to look elsewhere for information. Many portfolio strategists have commented on the increased volatility the investment markets have experienced in the last two decades. It is quite possible that this increased access to data and information may cause some to take action and trade more frequently than they might have ordinarily. The introduction of new investment vehicles may also have had an impact.

So where do you look for data, information, and maybe even some wisdom? At my firm, independent research is highly valued, and we pay a fee for it. We also receive and listen to the research of major wirehouse and banking firms, such as JP Morgan and Goldman Sachs, but we use this information carefully and always consider that their slant may be biased due to pressure to meet sales goals. The goal of an investment bank's research is to create trades or transactions. That's where they make their money. So it should not come as a surprise that an urgent call to action is part of what they do to support their sales professionals, also known as brokers, advisors, or by other titles. As a firm, we place great value on services where the only revenue to the firm is the revenue from the fees we pay for advice. These services are can be expensive for the individual investor; some are in the five-figure range. One of the services we use is Ned Davis Research located in Venice, Florida, and another is Advisor Intelligence from San Francisco. There are many to consider and the process of selecting these is just as important as selecting individual investments.

A reasonable question is, "Shouldn't you do all your own analysis and save a lot of money?" It depends on your perspective. I value the work that other firms do and appreciate that their thinking may at times challenge my own. If my thinking is not challenged, then how could it possibly be valued? More importantly, how can I be sure that I haven't allowed myself to be deluded into a line of thinking that will not engage the result that is desired?

> ## Third Horseman Clues
>
> Independent research is the best weapon in fighting off the third horseman, Group Think. This accounts for what I've called the "Sea of Sameness," where the investment offerings look and act the same. Independence does have a price, but it is worth paying for by the investors willing to put in the work.

At the same time, a maniacal focus on data may be unproductive. Designing a portfolio also requires something else. Illustrative of this may be a concept Malcolm Gladwell used in a *New York Times* article he wrote. A portion is excerpted here.

As Gladwell writes, "Mysteries require judgments and the assessment of uncertainty."

From the *New Yorker:*

The national-security expert Gregory Treverton has famously made a distinction between puzzles and mysteries. Osama bin Laden's whereabouts are a puzzle. We can't find him because we don't have enough information. The key to the puzzle will probably come from someone close to bin Laden, and until we can find that source bin Laden will remain at large.

The problem of what would happen in Iraq after the toppling of Saddam Hussein was, by contrast, a mystery. It wasn't a question that had a simple, factual answer. Mysteries require judgments and the assessment of uncertainty, and the hard part is not that we have too little information but that we have too much. The C.I.A. had a position on what a post-invasion Iraq would look like, and so did the Pentagon and the State Department and Colin Powell and Dick Cheney and any number of political scientists and journalists and think-tank fellows. For that matter, so did every cabdriver in Baghdad.

The distinction is not trivial...

If things go wrong with a puzzle, identifying the culprit is easy: it's the person who withheld information. Mysteries, though, are a lot murkier: sometimes the information we've been given is inadequate, and sometimes we aren't very smart about making sense of what we've been given, and sometimes the question itself cannot be answered. Puzzles come to satisfying conclusions. Mysteries often don't.

Portfolio design requires a fair amount of judgment because it takes on the characteristics of a mystery, where not everything is indeed factual. In reality there are some things we do not know, nor can know. There still remains a need for the data to be filtered through one's experience and training. Assumptions need to be made. That is why valuations are so critical, and I've devoted an entire chapter to providing at least a basic framework on valuations and using this data in forming a judgment about true value. A price-to-earnings (P/E) ratio is in fact just another piece of data. That recognition is important, but that knowledge is likely more of a relational fact than one that can be used in an absolute fashion. Pure data in the hands of an amateur can be the investment judgment equivalent of giving a loaded pistol to a five-year-old. Appropriate judgment would suggest the five-year-old can't handle the responsibilities of a gun. Good call! In the investment context, judgment needs to be employed to use the data effectively.

> ## Fourth Horseman Clues
>
> Global displacements and transformations by their very nature present challenges to the way we assess and process information. In investing there are few absolutes, and treating the process like a puzzle will lead to frustration and disappointment.

The danger of the third horseman, Group Think, (also referred to as the sea of sameness) is exemplified by the notion that the investing marketplace has gone and continues to go through significant change. When I started in the financial advice industry in the mid-1970s, the choices basically came in four categories: stocks, bonds, open- and closed-end mutual funds, and unit investment trusts. In the nearly forty years since that time, exchange traded funds (ETFs) have come into being, taking a significant share of retail investing's market share. Twenty-five years ago, ETFs didn't exist; now there are more than 1,500 ETF/ETN[6] listings currently being traded. This has provided investors not only with access to different types of markets; it has also presented the investor with intra-day trading opportunities to buy and sell.

---

[6] Exchange Traded Notes are similar to ETF's in that they track an index. The difference is no distributions in the form of dividends come from ETN's

While intra-day trading is contraindicated for long-term investing, it does provide some comfort for some people. Some may immediately think of the opportunity to "get out" when the market is high and "buy in" when the markets are low. This is commonly referred to as the ability to "time the market". The notion of "timing the market" (See Chart on facing page) has been around forever. It is an example of a bad idea that just won't go away. Undoubtedly, you get letters, newsletters, and e-mails claiming to have a "proven" system for timing the markets. The notion of market timing is very compelling. Who wouldn't want to be able to capture only the gains in the market and avoid the losses? Personally, I have been on the search for the perfect market timing process for nearly forty years. Sadly, every system I have explored and tried has led to disappointing results. The outcome for me has been more "experience" of ideas that simply don't work. When the topic comes up I indicate we have an open job offer to anyone who can successfully time the market. The pay is great, and you don't even need to show up for work. Just call us up with the signals. Of course, you need to have a proven track record with actual trades over a period of time. So far, no takers. Just think about it. When you think of great investors, who on the list is a market timer? Warren Buffett? Peter Lynch? No. The great investors are not market timers. (More on that in the next chapter.) The emotional pull to engage in that activity is an example of some things that never change and should be avoided.

Things to do and watch for...

Despite all the hard evidence that market timing doesn't work, and the fact that there are no market timers who have been successful over long periods of time, the desire to engage in this practice continues. This is further evidence that humans are emotional beings and suppressing certain concepts is very difficult.

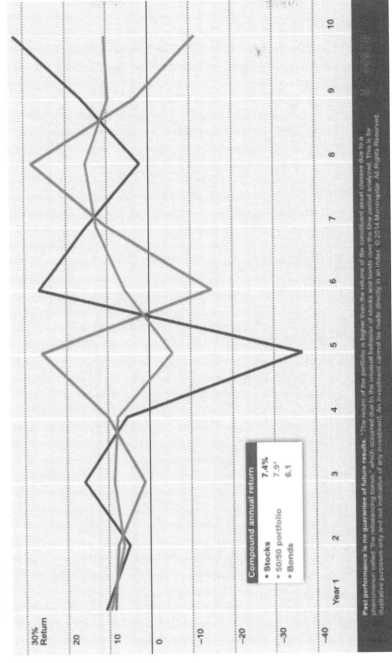

The Case for Diversifying
2004–2013

Compound annual return	
• Stocks	7.4%
• 50/50 portfolio	7.9*
• Bonds	6.1

@Morningstar 2014 – See Important Notice in Appendix page 162

Another significant change is that the scope of the investing environment has expanded dramatically. While the world was clearly on the march toward globalization forty years ago, in the investing world, at least in this country, investors stayed focused on the opportunities close to home. Frankly, this was true all over the world. Surveys show every country tends to have a home-country bias. We like to invest in what we are familiar with. Over time, we gain more visibility to investment opportunities outside our borders.

Global shifts, displacements, and transformations (also known as the fourth horseman) are not new. As recently as the late 1800s, Great Britain was considered the greatest economic power on the globe, and the United States was an emerging market. This was not the first time a global shift in economic power occurred. One can consider the Greeks and Romans and even China at an earlier time. Change is constant, and the new emerging markets of Brazil, Russia, India, China, and South Africa, known as the BRICS, are growing in significance and power. The growth of these economies (assuming the growth continues) will have a dramatic impact on who will eventually be the world's reserve currency and wield economic power. I've found some US citizens feel threatened by the notion that some other part of the world can exercise its economic influence, but as history teaches us, such shifts have happened before and probably will happen again.

Fourth Horseman Clues

Increased globalization (the fourth horseman) and the changes that it brings, not only economically, but also geopolitically, will continue their march, presenting many changes to the world's population. Consumerism is spreading to parts of the world that even a few years ago we considered impossible.

The financial services world has and will continue to change dramatically. It was not too long ago that commissions were a standard part of every transaction, and the commission rates were fixed across all firms. Commissions were deregulated in 1974, and change began to accelerate. Before that time the large brokerage firms controlled the brokerage fees that were mandated for everyone to use. After deregulation, consumer choices began to blossom. First, when competition came into vogue, it spawned new firms, such as Charles Schwab, TD Ameritrade, and Fidelity, whose business proposition initially was that they could effect trades at a lower cost. This immediately attracted those who wanted to act as "do it yourselfers" and place their own trades. This ultimately placed pressure on the big wirehouse brokers to compete. Of course, they emphasized their "full service," but some investors did not want or need full service. They wanted to lower their costs!

Charles Schwab was an innovator in another area, serving investment advisory firms. The independent registered investment advisor firm existed prior to deregulation (at the time called the "Big Bang"), and they used large wirehouse brokers and banks to place trades and custody assets. Since the number of players was limited and regulated, the price to provide these services was not insignificant. Many independent advisors placed trades, and the customer/client would receive a statement from each mutual fund he or she held. This resulted in a massive amount of paper flowing to the investor. In addition, there was not a convenient way to charge a fee to the account, and so mutual funds that carried a sales charge, or "load," were very common. Although no-load funds had come into existence, they had a very small share of the market. After all, a broker couldn't make a living selling those. The sales load on a mutual fund was almost always a standard 8.5 percent, which by today's standards is almost unheard of. In addition, for smaller accounts, contractual plans existed. The contractual plans would often have a higher sales load, or expense, in the beginning, allowing small investors to make monthly payments rather than meet the minimum cost of $1,000. The upfront sales charges were often 20 percent the first year, 18 percent the next two years, then 8 percent for one year, and then 4 percent for the next twenty years. It would take years to break even. Even though the no-loads had a huge advantage, no one knew how to buy them and the professionals couldn't figure out how to easily get paid, so inertia won the war against change.

When Schwab introduced its institutional division that traditional cost structure changed and changed rapidly. Now advisors could implement a diversified portfolio of no-load funds, provide a consolidated custody report, and facilitate their fee payments. Probably nothing accelerated lower costs and transparency as much as the discount brokers providing a service platform to the truly independent, fee-only registered investment advisors.

As a side note, even the life insurance industry was affected by greater visibility and transparency with regard to cost. About the same time, the concept of universal life came into being. It showed the cost assumptions for mortality costs, expenses, and investment returns. Over time the increased transparency served consumers extremely well, fostering increased competition and lowering costs.

The increased availability of hedge funds is part of the changing world of investing. More time will be spent on the specifics of hedge funds and other alternative strategies in Chapter 9. Traditionally, hedge funds have been structured as private partnerships, limited partnerships, and limited liability corporations. The first hedge fund is thought to have been created in 1949 by Alfred W. Jones. For most of the time since then, the hedge fund space has generated lots of different "flavors," or investing strategies, and was reserved for those who held the status of accredited investors. *Accredited investor* is a termed divined by the US Securities and Exchange Commission (SEC) and generally refers to someone who has a million dollars or more in investable assets, excluding personal residences and has the sophistication to invest in private partnerships of this nature. Of course that limits the numbers of individuals that have the ability to invest but that has not stopped the proliferation of new hedge funds, and now many mutual funds are implementing hedge fund–like strategies.

Both hedge funds themselves and their mutual fund cousins attempt to provide strategies that provide more consistent or "absolute" returns than the "relative to the market" returns offered by the traditional equity markets. While some do, you must exercise extra caution and due diligence prior to investing. I remember a hedge fund expert at a recent investing forum who said, "All the smartest people in the investment business run hedge funds, but not all the people in the hedge fund business are smart." The attraction of earning large fees encourages a lot of players into the hedge fund world. Many don't make it past five years. Some never get to the level of invested capital to keep a fund operational. Others fade away because the performance has not lived up to expectations.

Often a prospective client will say, "I just can't keep up with all the changes in the investing world," or "There are just too many choices!" With more than five thousand stocks listed on major exchanges, 1,500+ ETFs, more than seven thousand mutual funds (yes, more mutual funds than stocks), and three thousand hedge funds in the United States, investors certainly have considerable choice in the market place. Because no one can effectively know about all these choices, in later chapters we

> ## Things to do and watch for...
>
> One would reasonably surmise that with so many choices the consumer of investment products has lots of choice. This can be true for the investor who does his or her research and discerns the differences. But "group think" is prevalent, and investors need to be on the watch in constructing portfolios.

will explore using screening tools and other criteria to shrink the universe to a more manageable level.

With increased choice comes more complexity. Add in the availability of seemingly infinite amounts of data and overlay that with varying and competing views of what all this may or may not mean, and the result is a world of investing that has become ever more daunting and requires well-defined processes and the discipline to carry out the work on a regular and ongoing basis. As human beings we all look for the "easy button," and the investing world is all too happy to provide the *appearance* of a simple and easy way. In a fast-changing world, having an easy button is compelling, but the good things in life for most of us never come easy. As Warren Buffett has said, "Investing is simple but it is not easy." That quote recognizes that solid principles can guide your way, but the hard part is finding the real nuggets among the sea of data that is irrelevant to an investor's needs.

CHAPTER 3

SO WHAT DOES WORK?

In investing, what is comfortable is rarely profitable.

—*Robert Arnott*

What I have found is that most investors would be happy with any investment that gives them a 10 percent guaranteed return that is tax-free. Of course, if that were obtainable, they would likely want more.

Of course, we all find the idea that we want high returns and no risks humorous at one level, but likely, since we find some truth in the notion. The investment markets are driven by fear and greed with human motivations at the core of any significant movement in the markets, up or down. And yes, this propensity to satisfy our human urges to avoid fear and pain or to experience pleasure drives all kinds of less-than-productive behaviors. (More in Chapter 8 about the impact of human behavior on investment returns.)

Experienced investors recognize that high returns with no risk are not only unlikely but are a cause to be suspicious of any idea that is presented showing high returns with no risk. A better proposition is to focus on portfolio design with the idea of increasing the probability of success in meeting goals and objectives. A "high probability" design increases the likelihood of meeting the goal. What are the key principles for having a high-probability portfolio? What I have found is that there are three prime functions in achieving a high-probability portfolio:

1. Valuations—not paying too much for an asset;

2. Diversification—not believing you are so smart that you "know" the best investment;

3. Rebalancing—a process to sell high and buy low on a regular basis.

Chapter 6 presents more information about valuations. Of course, buying assets at a good price always makes sense. Without attention to value, investors sacrifice good returns for suboptimal ones. For example, if you bought a condo (as I did) in 2006 and paid fair market price, seven or eight years later, you may be just getting back to even (or not). On the other hand, if you purchased the condo in 2010 (a more financially astute move), you would likely be showing a significant profit by now. Now, if the condo purchase were strictly for investment purposes, your return on investment would be nonexistent when you factor in the ongoing costs for real estate taxes, maintenance, and other costs.

Rory Corrigan, planning associate at White Oaks Wealth Advisors, Inc. in Minneapolis, likes to say, "Never love something that can't love you back." This statement is clearly appropriate beyond the investing world, but is especially relevant with regard to investing. Frequently, I encounter people who have attached themselves emotionally to their investments. "That stock got me where I am today," or "My dad (mom, grandfather, aunt, uncle) gave me that as a gift." The ultimate truth is that *you* may care, but clearly the stock, company, or building does not give a whit in any shape, manner, or form about your feelings. It is always helpful to be emotionally detached from investments and investing decisions. Most bad investment decisions are emotional ones. Save your emotional attachment for someone who can love you back. The investment won't!

One of the challenges for investors is that there is an exciting story for every investment idea. No story...no reason to take action. No exceptions! As human beings we all like "stories" and the story is often compelling. Unfortunately, in reality, there are at least two story lines and likely multiple stories for each investment. Determining which stories are realistic is often challenging and part of an intelligent due-diligence process. I always like a good story, but when it comes to investing, I need to discount the story, no matter how compelling it is, because *the value* is what will pay me back, not the story. Ultimately, the relative value in context with similar investment opportunities is paramount in sifting out the "story" from the reality.

Few would argue against the benefit of spreading your risk. It only makes sense to not place all your "eggs" in one "basket," but the temptations to do just that are often overwhelming. Tom and Sally learned this the hard way. Both Tom and Sally had senior management positions in separate publicly traded corporations. Tom's employer had been doing very well. The company was in the highly favored technology sector. Life was good! Tom had been granted a series of stock options, which had done very well—so well, in fact, that Tom and Sally would exercise or buy the stock options and hold the stock because they believed in the company so strongly. Over time Tom and Sally accumulated several million dollars of investable net worth, with over 90 percent of it in Tom's employer's stock. And why not? Tom knew the company very well and was very comfortable with its long-term prospects.

Then the unexpected happened. Suddenly earnings reports had surprises that showed results less than investment analyst had forecasted. The investment analysts forecasts of earnings were revised severely downward, and the same volatility that Tom and Sally had enjoyed on the upside was now working against them. Tom and Sally also faced a significant tax bill that year, because the latest option grant was a taxable event. They planned on selling some stock to pay the tax bill later. To complicate things further, the favored technology sector was no longer favored. They were forced to sell all their stock just to pay the tax bill as the stock declined 80 percent in value. The IRS doesn't take sad stories as payment.

Second Horseman Clues

There are many tools for warding off the evils of the second horseman, volatility, and certainly not putting all of your eggs in one basket is the foundation.

Loss is a difficult thing to bear. Whether the loss is because of a death, divorce, or a financial downturn, people go through five separate and distinct stages as they process and deal with the emotional process of a loss. The emotional response to these five steps often causes investors to make decisions they are later unhappy with. The stages one goes through after suffering a financial loss may look something like this:

The first is denial—a feeling of "This can't be happening!" Then comes anger: "The market analysts have it wrong!" or "This isn't happening!" or "Maybe I need to check the quote on a different service." After a while the reality does start to sink in, and then comes the bargaining stage: "What if I tried this instead?" or "I must have some other choices!" Bargaining can turn some to prayer or even threats.

Of course, the likelihood of any bargaining being effective is slim to none. More recognition leads some to the next stage: depression. Of course, losing a few million dollars is not supposed to be a positive feeling, is it? Yet, depression seldom leads to sound decision-making, either. One needs to get to the next stage, acceptance, to finally be able to make effective choices. Should we hold on or sell, and how will a plan to move forward be put in place?

While these five stages need to be traveled through in order for the person to move on, if the person had not placed such a huge bet to begin with and had spread the exposure to risk in several categories, the loss could have been avoided or at least mitigated significantly. As the Kenny Rogers song goes, "Know when to hold 'em, and know when to fold 'em."

It may be true that the quickest way to get wealthy is to not diversify. Yet the easiest way to get poor is to not diversify. Bert and Alice believed in diversification, or at least they thought they did. They owned ten mutual funds and felt they had followed all the rules. The funds were picked from a financial magazine that touted them to be the best funds to own *now* ("now" being 1995)! What Bert and Alice did not appreciate was that all the funds were large-cap US stock funds. They got hit hard in the 2000 downturn, but they didn't pay much attention since they were both working at the time. The market and their value recouped by 2007. Then the Great Recession hit. Their account values plunged 50 percent. This time, being retired, they felt this drop more significantly. They had to do something, so they sold and went to cash, locking in their losses. Six years later, they now recognize that selling was a terrible move. While they preserved the amount of money they had, they had left the possibility of recouping their investment off the table. If they had built a true multi-asset class portfolio, they would have lost far less. Their loss of 50 percent meant they needed 100 percent growth to get back to even. While this did in fact happen over time, they feared it would be near impossible to accomplish. If they had diversified appropriately, the climb to recovery would have been less steep and they may have been able to stay in the game rather than folding in the depression stage.

The Retirement Dilemma

People's attitudes do change when they are relying on their portfolio for their income. No longer having a paycheck coming in heightens the sense of risk within a portfolio. This can cause some investors to be too conservative in their allocations, making it harder to meet their objective over the long term. It can even cause some investors to give up even trying. A strong diversification policy can go a long way toward reducing risk and preserving the rate of return needed to meet long-term needs.

Portfolio rebalancing is a topic that ultimately is so simple to talk about but hard to implement. It is truly hard to sell your best-performing investments and invest more in positions that have not been doing as well, but this approach has proven its value in moderating risk and enhancing returns over the long term.

In effect, rebalancing is a tactic that forces an investor to buy low and sell high. Some experts would argue that portfolios should be rebalanced frequently, such as every month. Others say to rebalance as necessary, such as when an asset class is over weighted by 10 to 20 percent. In a paper titled "Opportunistic Rebalancing: A New Paradigm for Wealth Management," Gobind Daryanani, CFP®, PhD, says the optimum time to rebalance is when an asset class is out of balance by 20 percent. The net impact of doing this adds, on average, 0.5 percent per year in additional returns. It is easy to scoff at 0.5 percent per year, but it will truly add up over time (see the next table). Let's assume an 8 percent return for a non-rebalanced

> ### Things to do and watch for...
>
> It is also important to "know your number." Why would anyone take excessive risks when the risk of losing is greater than the risk of winning? If your nest is or very close to being "feathered," why risk it all? Know how much it will take to meet your short- and long-term needs. Isn't that enough?

portfolio and 8.5 percent for a portfolio that is rebalanced over ten, twenty, thirty, and forty years.

Time	Non-rebalanced	Rebalanced
10 Years	$2,158,925	$2,260,983
20 Years	$4,660,957	$5,113,046
30 Years	$10,062,656	$11,558,251
40 Years	$21,724,521	$26,133,015

Even small percentages add up over time. Rebalancing is a simple and easy way to reduce risk and add return over time. You just need to do it consistently.

Often I hear people pooh-pooh these three concepts of valuation, diversification and rebalancing yet these are the building blocks of a high probability portfolio. Those who ignore these three building blocks are relying on the stories they are being told and hoping for them to pan out and with a great reward. Sometimes they do, and sometimes they don't. I've seen my share of get-rich-quick stories, but the vast majority of successes in accumulating significant wealth were due to sound portfolio design and focusing on value.

CHAPTER 4

SIX CRITICAL QUESTIONS
FOR EVERY INVESTOR

I think that the first thing is you should have a strategic asset allocation mix that assumes that you don't know what the future is going to hold.

—*Ray Dalio*

The individual investor should act consistently as an investor and not as a speculator.

—*Ben Graham*

We are confronted with choices in every phase of our life. Whether it is in how we treat others, whether to follow rules and laws, or how we control our health through diet and exercise, we need to make some choices. The hardest choices to make are often those for which there is more than one reasonable or acceptable course of action. For example, I can choose this diet, or another. Yet, at the same time, the abundance of choices may deter me from moving forward with a plan. In most cases, one of the courses of action is probably better than inaction.

In my work over the past four decades, I've learned that six questions can start investors on the right path or shine a bright light on why things may not be working with a particular portfolio strategy. It may seem like there is an obvious answer to some of the choices, but it is only obvious to you in the context of your situation. Reasonable and intelligent people can and do answer the same questions differently based on their skills, interests, time commitments, and other factors. Let's take the questions one by one.

Either we know or we don't know...

Do we know all we need to know? It would seem that in a world with 24/7 news coverage on financial topics and a bevy of people at cocktail parties all seeming to know what we should know. The answer for this is *we must know*! Yet, as a professional who is studying the markets all the time, I recognize that in fact I *don't* really know what is going to happen. In fact, most of the data that is presented for our consumption consists of conflicting opinions, and is not a locked-in-stone fact. Of course, the "information" may give a sense that we as investors "must act," but in reality that is most likely not the case.

Those of us who are getting a little long in the tooth will remember the days before the proliferation of hundreds of news channels. The news was consumed at noon, six, and ten (central time), and it was limited to thirty minutes. Now we have 24/7 news coverage on dozens of channels, but do we have any more true knowledge or wisdom? That is questionable. A famous quote by Coach John Wooden, famous basketball coach for UCLA —"Don't confuse activity with achievement"— comes to mind. In a later chapter, we will explore in more depth how investors are sometimes their own worst enemies. Data and information is often at the core.

We have come to the conclusion that we can't know everything; therefore, we diversify for multiple scenarios. What has truly separated great investors from the "also-rans" has traditionally been a focus on value and not believing that they have all the answers. The knowledge that the great investors do not focus on the day-to-day noise in the markets, but the long-term intrinsic value in an investment. Investment geeks tend to use the term "asymmetrical risk profile," which means that the number for downside risk is minimized and the probabilities are more aligned for positive outcomes. (Of course, there are no guarantees, but we'll talk more about this in later chapters.)

Do you want to focus on average, accepting the good with the bad (indexing), or do you want to focus on finding the best investments (active)?

This question is one I typically characterize as the "Great Debate" within the investment community. There are reasoned arguments on both sides, and frankly, I don't believe there is a perfect right or wrong answer.

The proponents of the indexing or passive approach are in effect seeking to be at least average. This means that the effort is designed to have both underperforming securities as well over-performing securities. The proponents of this method of investing argue that 80 percent of managers do not outperform their index. So average is not the 50th percentile; it is the 80th percentile. One might think that this doesn't make sense. This is very true and the natural outcome. The 80/20 rule is nothing new. Commonly known as the Pareto Principle, the fact that this exists should be of no surprise. Whether in sports, entertainment, or business, 20 percent of players commonly are exceptional and 80 percent are not. We all want to be like the people in Garrison Keillor's *Prairie Home Companion*, "where the women are strong, the men are good-looking, and the children are all above average." Our fears are based on the possibility that our portfolios are below average, and, of course, we want something better than that!

The real question is not whether or not the Pareto Principle exists in investing—of course it does! The question is whether or not a process can be developed to identify the 20 percent of managers who consis-tently are better than the average or index approach. For those who can-not or will not invest the extra time, cost, and energy to do the research, the passive or index approach will likely be a significant step up com-pared to mindlessly acquiring active portfolio assets piece by piece with-out a plan. The extraordinary man-ager can be found if an investor is willing to work and apply a consis-tent process over time.

Those who can acquire and put into place active management strat-egies that do outperform will, over time, do quite well. The margin does not have to be high to have a signif-icant benefit. Just a 1 percent additional return over a passive approach, net of fees, will go a long way in providing a significant benefit.

> ## Things to do or watch for...
>
> Successful active investing requires more work and at-tention on the investor's part. Consistent work and process-es can lead to the superior results investors are seeking. Evaluate your own interest lev-el carefully. Often it is not how smart you are but how diligent and process-focused you are.

The active versus passive debate will likely continue for as long as there are financial industry investment providers who benefit by being on one side or the other. Low-cost providers are not being altruistic in promoting the passive approach. They too are promoting a process that they hope investors will buy. Of course, there is nothing wrong with pro-moting what you do; it is just simply promotion, much like what the ac-tive providers are putting into the mix.

Maybe the best solution is not that you need to make an all-or-nothing choice, but rather that you need to use each style where it is best suited. This is the school of thought that many in the professional community follow in order to be agnostic in regard to this decision. The fees for active managers have to be earned through higher net after-fee returns. If they earn them, great! If not, a passive choice is a better option. In the largest, most liquid markets (more on liquidity later), a more passive approach is much harder to outperform. This is due largely to the extensive analyst coverage and the significant impact of index funds' (and closet indexers who are just trying to get close to the index) purchases to keep their portfolios matching the index itself.

Less-liquid markets, such as small-cap stocks, REITs (Real Estate Investment Trusts), and emerging and frontier markets have less analyst/market coverage, and the ability to exploit information is greater. This has given the active manager an edge, and many, including myself, believe that active management has a better-than-even chance of outperforming. That still means a significant amount of research is necessary to find the 20 percent, since the Pareto Principle lives in these asset classes as well.

I have the skills, passion, tools, discipline, and training to do the work.

A famous Steve Jobs quote is "The only way to do great work is to do what you love." Another spin by Harvey McKay is to "find something you love to do, and you'll never work another day in your life." This is particularly true of investing. Unfortunately, most investors treat investing as an episode in their life, not an ongoing body of work that needs to be done with diligence.

Take the case of Ben and Mary. Ben and Mary came in as prospective clients. They had accumulated a nice portfolio through saving and investing, worth several million dollars. Ben and Mary were great savers, and they regularly put excess cash flow into a portfolio of funds.

In reviewing their portfolio, I could easily tell—based on the group of funds they held in their accounts—that it was last looked at in the mid-1990s. (Sometimes I feel like an archaeologist on a dig when I review portfolios!) This group of funds had made all the lists as the best funds to own at that time. A couple of the funds were still fairly competitive, but the majority had seen better days.

Above-average portfolios are not reviewed occasionally. They are reviewed and tweaked consistently. Sometimes people rely upon—and I think a lot of times misinterpret—the concept of being a "buy and hold" investor. "Buy and hold" does not mean "buy and ignore." Few would dispute that themes and situations change quickly in our world today. To the "buy and ignore" investor "buy and hold" means that all investments that were good will be good forever. Nothing could be further from the truth! Buy and ignore is just plain dangerous and hazardous to your wealth.

It is important to understand ourselves and what we are drawn to do. A personal example is that I am the world's worst handyman. I am good at a lot of things, but when I go to get a hammer, wrench, or pliers, my friends and family find all kinds of excuses to leave the area for their own safety and well being. While many people not only enjoy doing small household repairs and projects and may even think of them as a form of therapy, I just plain lack the skill and patience to do these kinds of projects. For me, they are just torture!

Those who recognize their skills and passions tend to do well in those pursuits, and wisely find another way to get other tasks done.

Investing can be approached in many ways, but in the end it requires consistent, regular attention and process. If you have the interest and commitment, then you may be your best advisor. If you lack the consistent, regular, and disciplined focus, then you as your best advisor may be a "not so much."

Should I focus my investments or diversify?

As stated earlier, the quickest way to get rich is to not diversify, and the quickest way to get poor is to not diversify. The example of Bert and Alice in Chapter 3 demonstrates the unfortunate consequences of not recognizing the benefits of diversification. Many think that when it comes to investing diversification is synonymous with the stock market. Personally, the word *investing* is much broader to me. Lately I have been hearing, "I don't want to invest right now. The 'market' is too expensive." Effective diversification incorporates more than just the stock market and a market value focus leads an investor down the wrong path.

What these people really mean is that they don't like that the indexes in the stock markets are at or near new highs, they are concerned that the market will have a significant pullback, and believe that a better time to invest is on the horizon. Chapter 6 will show how this assumption is almost always wrong. But wait, you might be thinking, isn't investing more than just the stock market? Isn't the decision to leave money in cash an investing decision? Ultimately, the question is whether or not it is a good investing decision. Leaving money in the money market account is an investing decision. Likely a poor one, based on the evidence, but a decision nonetheless.

In every investment decision, a risk of some type is assumed. Most investors focus all their attention on volatility or the potential fluctuation of the investment. In some sense they are concerned with an absolute loss of capital, which, of course, makes sense. While fear and greed clearly drive movements in the liquid equity markets, it is fear that causes people to sell out at market bottoms and buy at market tops. There are multiple sources of risk for investors to consider, including volatility or market risk, interest rate risk, inflation, loss of capital, credit or default, foreign exchange rates, and geopolitical risk. Proper and comprehensive asset class diversification can mitigate these risks, but the one that most investors ignore or minimize is the risk of not offsetting inflation and thereby losing purchasing power.

Ike and Tina had accumulated a nice portfolio and had a business that was doing well. It wasn't a huge business but gave off a nice cash flow. They sold the business and invested all the proceeds in government bond mutual funds and CDs. Ike and Tina continued to live conservatively, but over time their real estate taxes went up and the utility bills went up, as did other costs. They had retired fairly young, in their late fifties. They really didn't think they would still be alive in their eighties, but here they were. As their costs went up, they eventually had to start taking money from principal as interest rates declined. Their account value dwindled until it became obvious they could no longer maintain the lifestyle they had worked so many years to attain. By ignoring inflation and interest rate risk, the lifestyle they had dreamed about gradually became impossible to maintain.

The graph on page 38 shows the relationship between inflation as measured by CPI and fixed-income returns. Fixed income investments, such as bonds and CDs, have historically been a poor choice to offset inflation. Focusing on one asset class always has its pluses

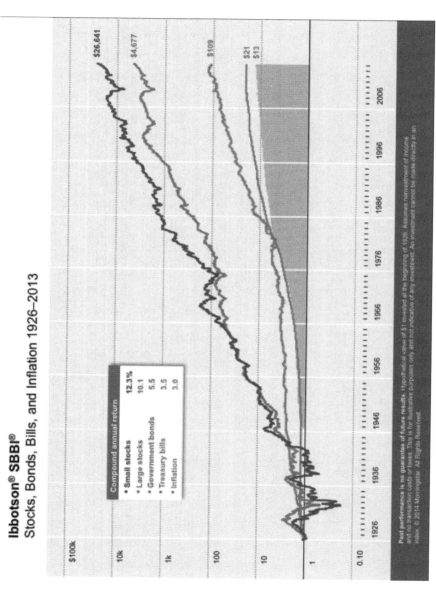

Ibbotson® SBBI®
Stocks, Bonds, Bills, and Inflation 1926–2013

Compound annual return

• Small stocks	12.3%
• Large stocks	10.1
• Government bonds	5.5
• Treasury bills	3.5
• Inflation	3.0

$26,641
$4,677
$109
$21
$13

@Morningstar 2014 – See Important Notice in Appendix page 162

and minuses, but in most cases it means increased risk in one of the eight risks types identified above.

Successful investors should consider a broad spectrum of risk when deploying capital. Well-diversified portfolios are the most effective strategy to obtain high-probability results.

What is more important, costs or results?

Occasionally I meet an investor who is totally focused on costs. But is the percentage of cost the most important criteria, or are the net results after fees more important? For me, the most important issue is the net result, not the cost. That does not mean that costs should be ignored or minimized in an intelligent process; instead, it means that an investment opportunity should not automatically be ruled out on costs alone. Think of it this way: Let's assume there are ten thousand opportunities and one hundred are the lowest cost. Should the other 9,900 be totally ignored, or should they at least be considered if they have in fact consistently added value? As mentioned earlier, the burden of proof with regard to effectiveness is on the manager with the higher expenses. To take the example further, Alex Rodriguez (A-Rod) is more valuable to the New York Yankees than I am. A whole lot more!

I think the answer is very clear. Focusing only on costs is a form of investment discrimination that may have a significant cost to you as an investor. Instead, cast as broad a net as possible. Selecting a few index funds is a shortcut answer that may dampen results.

CHAPTER 5

ASSET ALLOCATION DECISIONS

Investing should be more like watching paint dry or watching grass grow. If you want excitement, take $800 and go to Las Vegas.

—*Paul Samuelson*

The discussion about diversification in the last chapter suggested that many investors may think they are diversified when in reality they have funds or securities that will generally act in the same way when adverse economic and market events become apparent. The key to effective diversification is not just the number of securities. It is also having investments that will act differently than one another. In times of economic and equity market stress, the equity markets will often have a drawdown of some significance. At the same time, there is often a flight to quality (often treasury) securities, giving them a positive lift to their prices.

Asset allocation is a very confusing topic for many, not because it is so complicated, but because managers may describe several different methodologies and approaches to deploying assets. There are commonly three broadly accepted approaches: static, dynamic, and tactical.

A "static" asset allocation approach is much as the term suggests. It stays the same over time. The prescribed division between asset classes is established and gets rebalanced on a periodic basis. In its most basic form, one can think of the 60 percent equity, 40 percent bond/fixed income as a very basic example of this methodology. If equities were to increase to 65 percent, then the excess of 5 percent is moved from equities to bonds, bringing the balance of 60 percent equities and 40 percent bonds back to the original allocation. Over time more asset classes, such as international equities, REITs, and so forth have been added to some static approaches to end up with more "slices" in the pie chart. The static approach makes no effort to use judgment as to which asset classes are over- or undervalued relative to the others.

The "dynamic" asset allocation approach allows for over- and under-weighting allocations to specific assets for conditions the investor and/or advisor deems prudent. In this approach, the static model is often the starting point for a portfolio, but the strategy doesn't stop there. For example, an investor/advisor may have the view that international equities are overvalued relative to US equities. In that case, the investor/advisor will likely reduce the weighting of the international equities and add to the US equity holdings. Each asset class is evaluated on a regular basis for its relative valuation to the norm for evaluation. The dynamic asset allocation approach allows for more flexibility to be ready for trends on the horizon.

"Tactical" asset allocation can easily be confused with the dynamic methodology, but in many ways it is very different. Static and dynamic make no attempt to "time" the market, whereas the tactical approach is more about being in and out of the markets based on a short to intermediate view of market conditions rather than a long-term view of the markets. Logically, if we were able to do this successfully (and legally, with no insider trading), it would clearly be a compelling model. Buy only investments that are going up and sell all those that are about to decline. Cool! Unfortunately, a way to do this successfully hasn't been found. Of course, there are times when someone makes a great call on the market, and he or she receives a lot of recognition. But true success is not making a great call once, but making great calls consistently and regularly.

The cost of a wrong call is especially costly. Commonly known as being whipsawed, being in and out of the market at the wrong times compounds the net negative impact. In case you're reading this and you say "I have a great system that does successfully "time the market"" please let me know. The chart on page 44 shows the impact of missing the best month in any year and the

Third Horseman Clues

The third horseman, the group think/sea of sameness, is very dominant in asset allocation. Nearly every financial advisor will have an asset allocation pie chart in his or her arsenal of communication tools. Key questions to consider include:

1. Is this allocation the same or different than others you've seen?

2. What will this asset allocation strategy bring to the table that others don't?

3. Which assets will fight the three other horsemen in your portfolio?

corresponding negative impact on returns. It is easy to spot a trend that has already happened, but to be a successful market timer; you need to call the trend before it even happens. As referenced earlier, the essence of the asset allocation models that the financial services industry has promoted for many years

Market-Timing Risk
The effects of missing the best month of annual returns 1970–2013

- Annual return
- Annual return minus best month

Return if invested for the whole year

Return if the best month is missed

Past performance is no guarantee of future results. This is for illustrative purposes only and not indicative of any investment. An investment cannot be made directly in an index. © 2014 Morningstar. All Rights Reserved.

@Morningstar 2014 – See Important Notice in Appendix page 162

is based on the notion that 90 percent of investment returns are based on asset allocation, not security selection. Much of this has been based on a Nobel prize-winning paper titled "Portfolio Selection," by Professor Harry Markowitz, written in 1952. Professor Markowitz studied the returns of large pension funds to try and ascertain the reasons some funds performed better than others and discovered that the return differences were more attributable to the allocation of the fund than to the actual security selection of the fund. In other words, the markets are relatively efficient and the particular stock mattered less than the fact that there was an exposure to stocks. All the work was historical in nature and not intended to be prospective. To suggest that portfolio returns prospectively could be controlled by asset allocation simply was not and is not the case.

It is also important to keep in mind that in 1952, investing in international stocks and bifurcating stocks by small, medium, and large and between growth and value were not commonly accepted or implemented practices. So in most, if not all, cases, the allocation was between US stocks and US bonds. In one sense having more equity exposure makes intuitive sense based on the knowledge of the day, but it is also important to recognize that the returns from stocks and bonds weren't all that different in the time frame before Markowitz's paper was published. It is also interesting to note that in 1952 nearly half of the return from stocks came from dividends, a paradigm much different than the realities of the twenty-first century to date.

The Markowitz work gave an important start to how thinking evolved in the investment world. Important information from the paper gave professionals in the investing field and academics richer information to create better tools to design portfolios. With an expected return of an asset class, the asset classes' standard deviation statistic, and the correlation coefficient, you could model portfolios' risk and return characteristics and create a graph known as the "efficient frontier." It was so cool! Or at least I used to think so until the reality sunk in. It was a useful tool, some of the time, to show the downside risk of a portfolio, but it did nothing predictive with regard to how the portfolio in fact performed. Showing numbers with six digits to the right of the decimal point implied way more accuracy than the software products could possibly provide.

I felt cheated and misled about the whole "Modern Portfolio Theory" concept. While accurate when used in looking back in time (it did tell why the portfolio behaved the way it did), it did not help in constructing a new portfolio. The mathematical culprits were in two areas: the expected rates of return and the correlation coefficients. Both needed to be right, and both are nearly impossible to get right prospectively on a consistent basis. Here's why: we all know about GIGO, "garbage in, garbage out." Most portfolio optimizers based their estimate of future returns on a historical mean rate of return. Do the average returns for an asset class really inform us as to what to expect going forward? Maybe yes, maybe not so much. Investors make decisions that affect the returns on their portfolios. They take money (withdrawals) from the portfolio for children or grandchildren's education; they buy second homes and automobiles. They add money (make additional deposits) when they receive lump sums from bonuses, inheritances, or transactions from the sale of a business. The timing of all these transactions has an impact on the portfolio's return. (The impact of investor decisions on portfolio returns will be explored in greater detail in Chapter 8.)

In the end, using average returns is instructive but does not offer any real investing value. Another choice is to develop an estimate of asset class returns on your own or purchase them from a third-party firm. (Return expectation will be covered in more detail in Chapter 6.)

Another data point is the standard deviation of an asset class over time. Statistical terminology can seem mysterious to non-math geeks

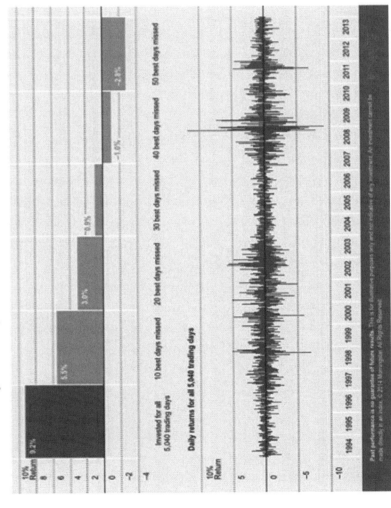

The Cost of Market Timing
Risk of missing the best days in the market 1994–2013

@Morningstar 2014 – See Important Notice in Appendix page 162

and a bit off-putting. In the end it is fairly simple. Standard deviation is a measure of the fluctuation up or down from a mean return. For example, if the long-term average standard deviation of a stock is 20 percent and the expected return is 9 percent, the stock is expected to go as high as 29 percent on the upside and -11 percent on the downside within two-thirds of the observations. In other words, it provides a range of returns and can be very helpful in understanding the expected volatility of an asset or group of assets in a portfolio. The standard deviation of an asset is fairly easily available through many services on the Internet.

The third critical component of portfolio optimization software is the correlation coefficients, or how assets act in relation to other asset classes. The goal is to find asset classes that have relatively low correlation to one other, as shown in the table on page 50. For example, the grid listing some asset classes is laid out both vertically and horizontally. The value in the first column, US large-cap stocks, has a correlation of 1.0 to itself. In other words, it acts exactly the same. And, of course, it should! It *is* the same. The lowest correlation at .005 is non-US bonds. So it is expected that non-US bonds will not act at all like US large-cap stocks and, consequently, offers some value as a diversifier to a portfolio. Another low-correlated asset is cash. Being a low correlation alone does not necessarily indicate that an allocation should be made. The asset allocation decision is more complicated than that.

It is also important to recognize that data shifts over time. In the case of correlations, it can shift suddenly and without warning. The financial crisis in 2008 is an apt example of how the data is instructive but not prescriptive. In the financial meltdown, the whole concept of diversification and asset allocation was called into question. During the crisis, there seemed to be no asset class—save short-term treasuries and cash—that provided any diversification. Corporate bonds sank in value just like stocks. The impact of the financial crisis was global; international allocations fell and provided no help, and in some cases, they were in a worse place than domestic allocations. Correlations had gone to one! In other words, everything had gone in the same direction with total disregard for historical correlations. The data simply didn't help.

Warren Buffett once said, "Beware of geeks bearing formulas." In other words, data helps most of the time, but not all the time. Just like in the science of meteorology, there is a significant body of knowledge and data, and they can get things right most of the time. Yet, just like the weatherperson's forecast, the element of surprise still occurs because there are many complex relationships, and these relationships and how they react to one another can change the outcome dramatically.

The beautiful thing about all this data is that it can be instructive in designing and developing a well-diversified portfolio that will perform reasonably well over time, and it can assist in recognizing the risk level of the portfolio and provide a fulcrum to lever this knowledge to elect appropriate asset classes and specific assets. The most dangerous thing about the use of software in asset allocation is that the results it spits out imply certainty. Spitting out charts and tables with data represented to, in some cases, the sixth decimal place may imply accuracy. Nothing could be further from the truth! The number of digits to the right of the decimal in data generated by software is not an indication of the reliability or preciseness of the data.

Correlation Matrix for the 14 Asset Classes

	U.S. Lg Cap Growth	U.S. Lg Cap Value	U.S. Mid Cap Growth	U.S. Mid Cap Growth	U.S. Sm Cap Growth	U.S. Sm Cap Val	Foreign Industrialized Mkts Stocks	Emerging Mkts Stks	U.S. Investment Grade Bonds	U.S. High Yield Bonds	Non-U.S. Bonds	Cash	Commodities	Real Estate
U.S. Lg Cap Growth	1.000	0.848	0.896	0.740	0.856	0.718	0.582	0.517	0.189	0.528	0.005	0.023	0.124	0.444
U.S. Lg Cap Val	0.848	1.000	0.778	0.899	0.743	0.844	0.586	0.537	0.230	0.577	-0.008	0.052	0.141	0.588
U.S. Mid Cap Growth	0.896	0.778	1.000	0.776	0.980	0.792	0.558	0.559	0.125	0.562	-0.019	-0.019	0.162	0.515
U.S. Mid Cap Val	0.740	0.899	0.776	1.000	0.767	0.957	0.536	0.512	0.212	0.620	-0.015	-0.002	0.150	0.678
U.S. Sm Cap Growth	0.856	0.743	0.980	0.767	1.000	0.805	0.539	0.560	0.097	0.581	-0.036	-0.035	0.161	0.541
U.S. Sm Cap Val	0.718	0.844	0.792	0.957	0.805	1.000	0.516	0.517	0.160	0.644	-0.032	-0.013	0.157	0.701
Foreign Industrialized Mkts Stocks	0.582	0.586	0.558	0.536	0.539	0.516	1.000	0.667	0.170	0.398	0.288	0.052	0.181	0.389
Emerging Mkts Stks	0.517	0.537	0.559	0.512	0.560	0.517	0.667	1.000	0.036	0.432	0.025	0.003	0.201	0.343
U.S. Investment Grade Bonds	0.189	0.230	0.125	0.212	0.097	0.160	0.170	0.036	1.000	0.382	0.447	0.237	-0.107	0.157
U.S. High Yield Bonds	0.528	0.577	0.562	0.620	0.581	0.644	0.398	0.432	0.382	1.000	0.082	0.010	0.039	0.499
Non-U.S. Bonds	0.005	-0.008	-0.019	-0.015	-0.036	-0.032	0.288	0.025	0.447	0.082	1.000	0.229	-0.076	-0.001
Cash	0.023	0.052	-0.019	-0.002	-0.035	-0.013	0.052	0.003	0.237	0.010	0.229	1.000	-0.163	-0.050
Commodities	0.124	0.141	0.162	0.150	0.161	0.157	0.181	0.201	-0.107	0.039	-0.076	-0.163	1.000	0.159
Real Estate	0.444	0.588	0.515	0.678	0.541	0.701	0.389	0.343	0.157	0.499	-0.001	-0.050	0.159	1.000

@Morningstar 2014 – See Important Notice in Appendix page 162

Choosing the proper asset classes to allocate is an important part of the asset allocation process. The correlation matrix above may seem comprehensive—and it does cover a number of asset classes; however, it is lacking in some areas. For example, what about some of the asset classes in the category sometimes referred to as "alternative assets"? These assets are not represented here. (We will take a deeper look at this category of investments in Chapter 10.) First, I would like to take issue with the "alternative assets" as an asset class.

Some investors view alternative assets as an asset class and treat it as such. This view assumes that all the strategies act and behave in the same manner. In fact, there are many strategies in the category of alternative assets, and all act and behave differently from one another. Private equity has different return streams and reacts differently from common stocks, real estate, or commodities.

		Correlation with US Stocks
US Large Blend		1.00
US Large Growth		0.98
US Large Value		0.98
US Small Blend		0.95
US Small Growth		0.93
US Small Value		0.94
International Developed		0.90
Emerging		0.81
US REITs		0.79
Commodities		0.48

The table above does treat real estate and commodities as separate and distinct asset classes; however, it ignores other asset classes, such as long-short equity, convertible arbitrage, distressed debt, private equity, venture capital, direct ownership of real estate (as contrasted with REITs), energy, precious metals, hedge funds of various types, and managed futures. Each can be a reasonable choice and should be considered as part of an intelligent asset allocation strategy. In general, many of these strategies behave very differently from long-only stock and bonds positions and can add diversification value to a strategic portfolio.

Much attention has been drawn to the large private university endowments, particularly the Yale endowment. For many years under the stewardship of David Swenson, the Yale endowment enjoyed superior investment returns, and much of the credit had been given to the endowment's increased exposure to nontraditional strategies.[7] Most recently, significantly more than 50 percent of the portfolio is in absolute return strategies, natural resources, private equity, and real estate.

> ## Things to do or watch for...
>
> Statistical data can be extremely compelling. Data featuring two to six (or more) digits to the right of the decimal point seem to imply a lot of certainty.
>
> Be cautious in evaluating data in a one-time series; the data can and does shift dramatically.

Although there are important differences between institutional endowments and private individuals, the one thing they do have in common is the desire to distribute income, most often 5 percent of principal, to meet current needs for the institution and, in the case of private individuals, to provide for themselves in retirement and maintain family wealth.

Alternatives bring more absolute or consistent returns to a portfolio. Everyone loves to have a 25 percent up year in the markets, but enthusiasm is much lower for a 20 percent down year. For many years

---

[7] Source: 2013 Yale Endowment Report, http://investments.yale.edu/images/documents/Yale_Endowment_13.pdf

some asset allocation practitioners have said to diversify, an investor should look at US large and small stocks as separate asset classes together with international and REITs. However, as the chart on page 51 shows, this simply has ceased to be true. The correlation between these assets classes has increased and the diversification value has diminished.

This increased correlation and volatility is an area of concern, especially for investors—whether individual or institutional—seeking to have access to their portfolios

Table 1: Expected Returns and Standard Deviations

Alternative Asset Class (representative index)	Expected Return*	Standard Deviation*
Domestic Equity (Russell 3000 TR USD)	12.63	18.80
International Equity (MSCI EAFE GR USD)	11.17	21.70
Long/Short Equity (Credit Suisse Tremont Long Shrt Eqty USD)	10.45	12.66
Market-Neutral (Greenwich Global HF Eqty Market Neutral)	10.22	5.58
Arbitrage (CASAM CISDM Merger Arbitrage USD)	10.38	8.57
Managed Futures (Credit Suisse Tremont Managed Futures USD)	6.84	12.69
Commodities (DJ UBS Commodity TR USD)	6.27	16.79
Global Infrastructure (S&P Global Infrastructure TR USD)	12.65	21.47
Private Equity (Cambridge Associates US Private Equity)	13.47	10.77
Frontier Markets (MSCI Frontier Markets GR USD)	15.41	33.46
Treasury Inflation-Protected Securities (BarCap Gbl Infl Linked US TIPS TR USD)	7.08	5.22
Emerging-Markets Debt (JPM EMBI Plus TR USD)	11.67	16.09
Aggregate Bonds (BarCap US Agg Bond TR USD)	8.64	7.13

*These annualized statistics are calculated using quarterly data over the longest available time frame for each representative index.

for cash flow. For example, if there were an investment that could provide an 8 or 9 percent return and the volatility were half of what was expected in the equity markets, would that be a good choice? Let's take a look at the chart above.

Note first the expected return and the standard deviation of the domestic equity as represented by the Russell 3000 (the top three thousand market traded stocks in the United States). It shows a 12.63 percent expected return and a standard deviation of 18.8 percent. Now scan down the table to other asset classes. First, let's stop at market-neutral. Hmm...a 10.22 percent expected return, but look at the standard deviation—5.58, or less than a third of the volatility across the broad market as measured by the Russell 3000. Then, going farther down the table to the private equity category, the story is even more interesting. The expected return is 13.47 percent (higher than broad market), and the standard deviation is nearly half at 10.77 percent. So why wouldn't people put all their money in private equity then? Lack of liquidity is a main reason. Few people want to tie up the majority of their money for several years, as is the case with private equity. Yet an allocation to this asset ups the game for the overall portfolio. (We'll take a closer look at alternative assets in Chapter 9.)

The interplay between risk, return, and correlation is important when allocating assets. While not precise, it can inform the work of portfolio development. The chart on the next page taken from the same article as the preceding table, shows the relationship of the risk and return characteristics of various asset classes. The farther to the left you go, the lower the level of volatility; and the higher on the chart, the better the return.

Having too narrow a scope in selecting asset classes in putting together a portfolio can be limiting. Considering nontraditional opportunities as part of a balanced approach may provide opportunities that will enhance the portfolio's returns and also help control risk.

As discussed in this chapter, asset allocation approaches have changed over time and the combination of science and art have presented challenges over the years. Knowing the limitations of different approaches can help investors understand what these approaches do well and what limitations still exist. Yet, although asset allocation has no predictive value, it does serve to understand the risk and potential of a portfolio much more clearly than the absence of such tools. Investors and financial advisors still need to think and make reasoned judgments in light of their individual history, education, and knowledge of the topic.

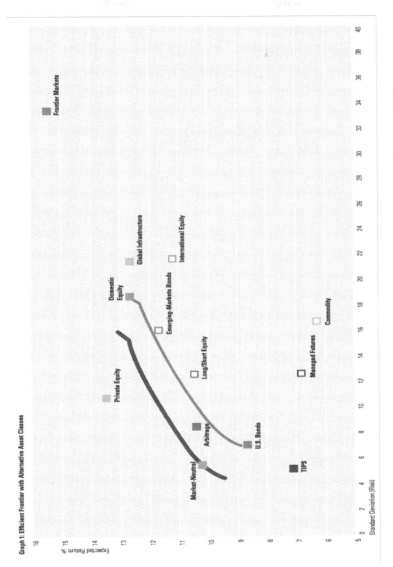

Graph 1: Efficient Frontier with Alternative Asset Classes

@Morningstar 2014 – See Important Notice in Appendix page 162

CHAPTER 6

IT'S ALL ABOUT VALUE

Price is what you pay, value is what you get.

—*Warren Buffett*

The stock market is filled with individuals who know the price of everything, but the value of nothing.

—*Phillip Fisher*

I n the previous chapter on asset allocation, during our consideration of the dynamic asset allocation methodology, the concept of value was brought up. How one determines value is an obvious key question that needs to be answered.

Jack watched the financial news every day. He loved the 24/7 financial news channels especially. When we worked out at the club, he was always tuning in. The first thing he would do when he got up in the morning and after getting home from work is flip on the TV. He felt really informed and smart about the goings-on in the markets. He would always be quick to throw out some quote he had heard that day. The sad news is that his portfolio was full of "tips" he'd heard, and it really wasn't doing all that well. What went wrong? Was he watching the wrong channel?

The financial news media constantly is referencing value: *This is overvalued! That is undervalued!* Of course, one expert's view is often contrasted with that of another "expert," leaving the audience to wonder who is right. In one sense, it is not important who is correct, since each may be representing a particular point of view or may have a financial interest in the answer. The main motivation for the financial networks is to sell advertising. There's nothing wrong with that, but to confuse that motivator with the idea that their role is to teach and inform may be dangerous to your wealth. The financial industry sometimes uses the term "financial pornography" to describe this financial information. It's designed to excite and encourage some kind of action with less than optimal results. The news media plays an important role, and nothing here should diminish that, but it is more important that a personal point of view on value is established and used consistently over time. Varying views of what value is will only lead to confusion.

Few people would dispute the notion that if you buy something at a low relative price and sell at an above-average price, then the end result is likely to be a favorable investment outcome. So simple, isn't it? Here is where the Warren Buffett quote at the end of Chapter 2 comes into play: "Investing is simple but it is not easy." The simple part is knowing that buying something cheap is often, but not always, good. The hard part is knowing what is genuinely cheap and what won't get cheaper. Clearly, some things are cheap because they are supposed to be. A failing investment is priced where it is for a reason, and the price may have generated more enthusiasm than appropriate.

There are two approaches in using a building block estimate of what a market could be expected to return over a period of time. One is based on expectations for GDP growth. For example, let's assume that the consensus view is 2.5 percent for economic growth in the United States. The dividend yield for the S&P 500 is 1.6 percent. When we add the two together, we arrive at a 4.1 percent expected growth, and we then add in a couple percent for average productivity gains, bringing us to 6.1 percent. Then the big wild card: the expansion or contraction of the price-to-earnings ratio. Using the S&P 500 as an example, the mean P/E ratio in May 2014 was 15.51 and the current P/E ratio was 18.66 at the same time. The chart below shows the P/E ratio since 1871. Fifteen times earnings is the norm. Clearly, the valuations, as shown on the

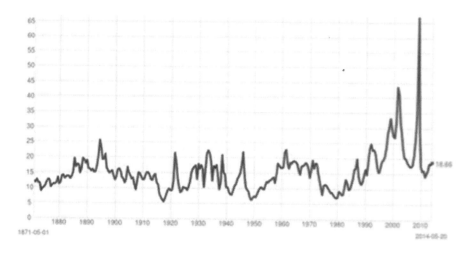

P/E chart, have been higher, but they are reaching a point that has marked market tops in the past. The bubble peaks in 2000 and 2007 clearly are much higher and, based on that, the P/E's could still expand significantly. Yet, to count on bubble-like valuations may seem less than prudent as well. Counting on significant P/E expansion at these levels requires a very high level of enthusiasm. So a reasonable outlook for the market is somewhere around 6 percent, assuming no P/E contraction.

On the other hand, the P/E contraction comes into play when the 6 percent number would be looked on as being too optimistic. Consumer confidence is a significant driver for the P/E contraction or expansion, which may be hard to gauge and is subject to sudden changes of events that may come from geopolitical events or other negative news. So what does this tell us about short-term performance? Not very much, it turns out, as overvalued markets can and do become even more overvalued. However, it is a pretty good indicator for long-term performance. Over five year periods of time, overvalued markets tend to perform under the mean return, and undervalued markets tend to perform over the mean return. The implications are important for over- and underweighting assets in an allocation plan. As mentioned above, normalizing earnings can enhance the valuation process.[8] Ed Easterling's work at Crestmont Research is instructive when it comes to developing a forward-looking view of the markets.

Mr. Easterling's work on secular equity markets shows the relationship between valuations and future returns. The chart on page 60 is from the Crestmont Research website (http://www.crestmontresearch. com/), graphically shows the relationships between high and low valuations when earnings are normalized. Clearly, buying at high valuations inhibits performance.

---

[8] Ed Easterling, Crestmont Research: http://www.crestmontresearch.com/, Author: *Probable Outcomes, Secular Stock Market Insights and Unexpected Returns, Understanding Secular Stock Market Returns*

SECULAR BULL & BEAR MARKETS PROFILE: 2013

Market Cycle From	To	(#) Total Years	Market	P/E Ratio Beg	End	Inflation Beg	End	(#) Positive Years	(#) Negative Years	(%) Positive Years	(%) Negative Years	Max Pos. Yrs In Row	Max Neg Yrs In Row	Avg Gain In Pos. Years	Avg Loss In Neg Years	Change Begin To End
1901	1920	20	BEAR	23	5	-2%	16%	9	11	45%	55%	2	3	30%	-17%	2%
1921	1928	8	BULL	5	22	-11%	-2%	7	1	88%	13%	5	1	24%	-3%	317%
1929	1932	4	BEAR	28	8	0%	-10%	0	4	0%	100%	0	4	n/a	-32%	-80%
1933	1936	4	BULL	11	19	-6%	1%	4	0	100%	0%	4	0	34%	n/a	200%
1937	1941	5	BEAR	18	12	4%	5%	1	4	20%	80%	1	3	28%	-16%	-38%
1942	1965	24	BULL	9	23	11%	2%	18	6	75%	25%	4	1	16%	-8%	774%
1966	1981	16	BEAR	21	8	3%	10%	9	7	56%	44%	3	2	13%	-15%	-10%
1982	1999	18	BULL	7	42	6%	2%	16	2	89%	11%	9	1	18%	-4%	1214%
2000	????		BEAR	42		3%		9	5	64%	36%	5	3	13%	-13%	44%
WEIGHTED AVERAGE BEAR (excluding 2000)										42%	58%	2.1	2.7	21%	-18%	-14%
WEIGHTED AVERAGE BULL										83%	17%	5.8	0.9	19%	-5%	810%

Notes: The index and returns reflect the Dow Jones Industrial Average at year-end from Dow Jones & Company. The P/E ratio is based upon the S&P 500 as developed and presented by Robert Shiller (Y-ee, Irrational Exuberance; Bull & Bear). Market reductions are based upon Crestmont's assessment of cycles using peak and trough P/E ratios, inflation trends, and other analysis. The presentation does not include dividends, taxes, inflation adjustments, or transaction costs.

RETURN PATTERN (Red = down year; Green = up year; #% = annual change in the index, starting and ending DJIA Index is presented on the ends of the rows)

1901–1920: BEAR	71																72
P/E Ratio																	
CPI: Inflation																	
1921–1928: BULL	72																300
P/E Ratio																	
CPI: Inflation																	
1929–1932: BEAR	300																60
P/E Ratio																	
CPI: Inflation																	
1933–1936: BULL	60																180
P/E Ratio																	
CPI: Inflation																	
1937–1941: BEAR	180																111
P/E Ratio																	
CPI: Inflation																	
1942–1965: BULL	111																969
P/E Ratio																	
CPI: Inflation																	
1966–1981: BEAR	969																875
P/E Ratio																	
CPI: Inflation																	
1982–1999: BULL	875																11497
P/E Ratio																	
CPI: Inflation																	
2000–????: BEAR	11497																
P/E Ratio																	
CPI: Inflation																	

Copyright 2003-2014, Crestmont Research (www.CrestmontResearch.com)

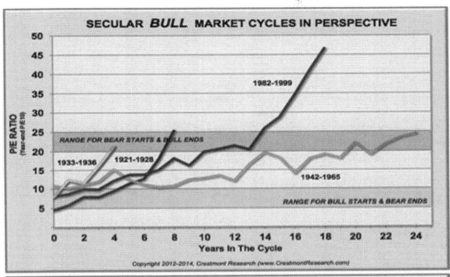

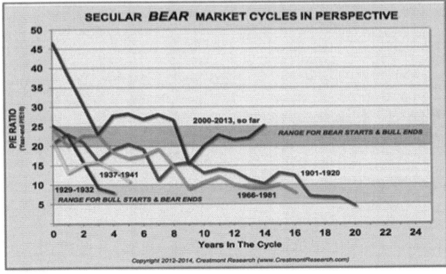

The second chart identified on page 61 breaks the trends down by secular bull and bear markets. Bull markets tend to start when valuations are low and end when they are high. While the short-term impact is that overvalued markets can and do get more overvalued, for the truly long-term investor, overweighting an overvalued asset class does not often fall into a high-probability success. So simple but not so easy.

Experience has taught me that to eliminate a particular asset class that appears to be overvalued or attempt to time the market during times like this does not work. If the short-term trend continues to go up in spite of overvaluation, an opportunity is missed. At the same time, having an over-weighted allocation to an overvalued asset class exposes a portfolio to more risk than necessary. Of course, the S&P 500 is but just one asset class, and others need to be considered.

There are many perspectives on value that should be considered. First, what is the current economic climate, and what is it expected to be in the short, intermediate, and longer term? The goal is not to "know the number" for gross domestic product, inflation, and interest rates, but to have a view that recognizes the trends that are in place and the relationship those trends may have to certain asset classes.

What is the building blocks methodology?

The building blocks methodology is a way of forecasting the returns on equities and fixed-income asset classes using the current risk-free rate and historical risk premiums.

The main idea is that the return investors should expect on asset classes should equal at least the return on a "riskless" asset, such as a one-year US Treasury STRIP, plus some risk premium for taking on additional levels of risk.

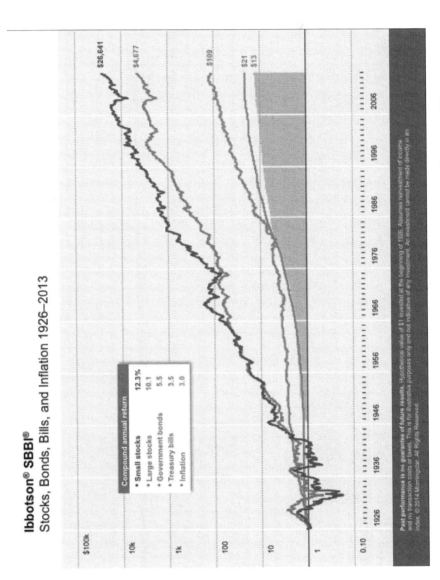

Ibbotson® SBBI®
Stocks, Bonds, Bills, and Inflation 1926–2013

Compound annual return	
• Small stocks	12.3%
• Large stocks	10.1
• Government bonds	5.5
• Treasury bills	3.5
• Inflation	3.0

$26,641
$4,677
$109
$21
$13

@Morningstar 2014 – See Important Notice in Appendix page 162

For example, it is riskier to invest in a large-cap stock than a one-year US Treasury Bill. Therefore, the additional compensation that investors expect for holding stocks as opposed to government securities is called the equity risk premium. It is calculated by taking the historical difference between the returns of the two asset classes.

The chart on page 63 will be our starting point. The inflation rate over the time period of 1926 through the end of 2013 is shown to be 3 percent. Over the same period of time, the Treasury bill rate is 3.5 percent. This half a percent spread is fairly constant over longer periods of time—for example, three to five years or longer. So if you have a view of inflation, it will be the base of your building block approach.

The same idea applies to other fixed-income asset classes. The following is an example showing how the expected return on a long-term corporate bond asset class may be forecasted: Expected Return = Risk-Free Rate (T-Bill) + Bond Horizon Premium (Longer-term bond yields) + Bond Default Premium. The horizon premium indicates that this is a long-term bond. Since long-term bonds are subject to interest rate risk, the risk premium is usually calculated by taking the difference between long-term government bonds and the US T-Bill total returns. The default premium is added to compensate investors for holding risky corporate as opposed to government bonds. The historical difference between government and corporate bonds with the same

First Horseman Clues

Using inflation as the base for a forecast is a great starting point and is helpful in evaluating asset classes on a comparative basis. If stocks are overvalued, an investor may make the judgment that the asset class may not meet the expectations to offset inflation as much as it has in the past. On the other hand, if the asset class is undervalued, one may conclude the asset class will do better than history.

maturity will give us this number. Using the long-term average of 5.5 percent, 2.5 percent over inflation and 3 percent over T-Bills will be a good number to use for a longer time horizon.

Before we go on, let's consider what has happened since 2000. Inflation has cooled to an almost nonexistent level, and interest rates have declined to historic low levels. Spreads on corporate bonds bring in the potential for default risk. Corporate bond spreads over Treasuries are usually 1 to 3 percent, so let's split the difference and call it 2 percent. If the difference (the spread) is too narrow then the perception of risk is low. In reality, low spreads are usually a warning sign that the winds are about to shift for the higher level of riskiness in bonds. Equity spreads over T-Bills have been relatively consistent over time at 6 to 6.5 percent over T-Bills. Again, relating to the markets since 2000, there have been many ups and downs with two very significant drawdowns of capital. That being said, the spread over the long term has roughly been 6 percent over T-Bills.

One can select a preferred outlook based on their work, consider how assets classes have performed in similar time periods, buy someone's opinion on the outlook, or use a building block methodology. One thing will be certain: Just like trying to predict the weather, the multitude of factors and the dynamics of their interaction are certain to vary. The key is to have a methodology and follow it. Jumping from one method to another each year will not lead to a successful portfolio design.

Next, having a view on the relative valuations of asset classes within and relative to various regions needs to be assessed. If a particular asset class is currently valued above its long term mean, this may suggest the asset class is overvalued. Various valuation indicators can be used, including current yield, price earnings ratios, price to book, price to cash flow, price to sales, price to earnings, and others. Often you might hear individuals focus on one or just a couple of these measures. I like to consider the entire body of evidence that can be gathered when assessing relative value.

Since some of the data is volatile in nature, some investors like to normalize earnings, offering a five- to ten-year time frame. While each method is not directly comparable to the other, each is a piece of the puzzle that needs to be considered.

Acquiring investments that are relatively undervalued traditionally has been a high-probability investment strategy for those with a long-term focus. It may take some time for valuations to be recognized, but when the valuations get back to normal, then above-average gains are realized in many cases.

Let's take a look at a few examples of various asset classes and what might be considered a "middle of the road" valuation from which we can make a judgment. A comprehensive look at all the various approaches is best saved for another book, but a few of the major ones can be explored here. Before we explore some valuation metrics, we must distinguish between strategies that are skill-based versus those that are market-based. For example, long-only strategies in the public equity and fixed-income markets are largely driven by the general direction of those markets. A manager can add value with security-selection techniques, but generally when a strategy in long-only equity markets is in a down market, the portfolio also generally goes down. As explored elsewhere in the book, portfolios may go down more or less based on the skill applied, but they do react in the same general trend as the markets they operate in.

But there are strategies that are more focused on playing with the cards that "Mr. Market" deals. Long/short managers are an example of such thinking. Overvalued stocks are shorted, and undervalued stocks are held long. The long/short managers really don't care about the direction "Mr. Market" is going in; their concern is that their strategy is making the best of the current situation. Other strategies, such as market-neutral, distressed debt, convertible arbitrage, and to some extent, private equity, are focused on value in a different and skill-based manner.

Long-only strategies do exist in a "relative" performance world and valuations *do* matter when it comes to long-term expectations. Overvalued asset classes are in effect "buying high." Value matters a great deal in "relative return" strategies. By using sound metrics as described in this chapter, you can make judgments about where you are in the investment cycle. Being overweight in equities when the markets are richly valued is not conducive to preserving or building wealth.

CHAPTER 7

THE PACKAGING OF INVESTMENTS

How many millionaires do you know who have be-
come wealthy by investing in savings accounts? I
rest my case.

—*Robert G. Allen*

The inside scoop on the business side of investment products: there is little question that investors in today's world have a multitude of choices. On one level, the choices seem overwhelming, and on another, the sameness of it all is tiring and does little to inspire the confidence to move ahead in a constructive manner. According to the 2013 Investment Company Factbook[9] there are more than 7,596 mutual funds. Oh! Just a minute—that only accounts for "open-end mutual funds," which offer shares continuously. There are also 1,194 ETFs and another 602 "closed-end funds" and 71,725 "unit investment trusts." As of the end of 2013,

---

[9] 2013 Investment Company Factbook, http://www.icifactbook.org/fb_data.html

there were 5,008 publicly traded stocks in the United States.[10] This is without limited partnerships, non-traded REITs, and other hedge fund structures. And this is just in the United States!

Third Horseman Clues

The marketing departments of the large financial institutions focus on what will sell, and what they can market effectively to the investing public. Decisions based on marketing appeal and, of course, compensation are all part of the process. Much of it is about packaging and less about whether or not the financial product will materially contribute something new and effective for the investing consumer.

The lowest rung in the investment ladder is the retail rung. The vast majority of advisors operating in the financial services industry are currently taking products off the retail shelf and using them to put together a portfolio that is intended to serve the client well. Retail investing is about packaging and volume. Investors and advisors in this world are faced with the same level of complexity and finding the differentiating elements of those products to be somewhat limited. Many of those associated with larger firms rely on the firm's "research" team to sort out the good from the less good, and therein the firm's "short list" is the source of all its wonderful investment ideas. All this sounds really good – a big firm, a "research" department." How could that go wrong? The best and the brightest are there, right? Maybe yes, maybe no.

When the sales of a particular brand of toothpaste start to slow, the first thing that is often done is to look at the packaging of the product and "update" its look to a more contemporary feel. Let's look at Jack's experience. Jack didn't like insurance products in general. He was familiar with annuities and generally disliked them for their expenses and

---

[10] http://online.wsj.com/news/articles/SB10001424052702304851104579363272107177430

the fact that they deferred income and did not have favorable capital gains treatment. Someone did get his ear one day and proposed a "new product" that would provide a guaranteed hedge against a down market in case he died and the market value was below his cost. Of course, upon further investigation, he found out this was just a new way of "explaining" a deferred annuity product. Usually the greater the hyperbole, the less the "new product" will be an optimum investment choice.

Investment products are necessarily part of the investing world. The rub is where product/distribution and advice may collide. In the early 2000s, our firm made the decision to use one of the larger firm's resources for selecting and implementing managers to be part of our clients' portfolios. The messaging was clear. We "large financial institutions" (LFIs) are big and can put more resources to the task. We LFIs have access to ideas that you don't or won't be able to use. We LFIs will constantly review and let you know when we find a better opportunity. Hmm…sounds pretty good, doesn't it?

After a couple of years, our firm evaluated the results as compared to the process we had in place prior to adding this approach. The differences were significant, and in spite of supposedly lowering overall fees in the "new and improved" way of investing, the process we had been using prior to this had performed significantly better than the "new and improved" way.

Why? Everything we had been told should have been a huge benefit to our clients, but the results told a different story. Why? It turned out there were three reasons: incentives, limited access, and stagnant research.

As it turned out, the most limiting factor was incentives. To be on an LFI's platform, a participating manager had to pay a fee to the LFI. This fee was a part of the fee the manager would have received in any case, and on the surface it seemed to be a nonissue. If "Really Cool Manager" (RCM) wanted to pay LFI a portion of his fee, what was the big deal? After all,

RCM doesn't have to deal with the end investor directly (less commitment) and is required to do less reporting. It turns out that the only managers that would agree to participate were those who really wanted to scale their business, and for whom that was the top priority. Marketing was their main focus, not investment results. Other managers refused the "pay to play" opportunity, and many of them were excellent managers whose focus was on the investment process, not on marketing and scale. It turned out that the "approved list" of the LFI had in effect needed to be approved by the "compensation department" (fictitious but, in effect, real) for approval to be on the platform.

> ## Things to do or watch for...
>
> Many investors don't see the multiple levels of fees in investment products. Questions about fees too often focus on only one level of costs.
>
> Key Questions:
>
> 1. What are the fees in this approach?
>
> 2. What are the "internal" fees beyond that?
>
> 3. What will be my "all-in" costs?

With regard to limited access, the starting point for most retail advisors associated with LFI was not the entire universe of investment options/products, but only those who would have enough scale to be considered. Therefore, a proven manager who may have reached a level of success may not have been considered because he or she had a seven-year track record, not a ten- or fifteen-year record, and, in LFI's eyes, didn't have enough current assets. Such requirements can be extremely limiting, as newer or emerging managers often do quite well and can add a lot to a portfolio.

The stagnant research piece included elements of the incentive and limited-access issues we just reviewed; however, it was also my sense that they knew very well who they wanted to sell and what they wanted. The ongoing research was focused on new money coming in and not the existing pool of assets. For example, Frank and Betty were direct clients of one of the LFIs and became disturbed when their results seemed to be different than the results published in LFI's marketing messages. When they discovered that their close friends, Sam and Bernie, had their portfolios there as well they found that very comforting. One day Sam, after a couple of beverages, remarked that they had the manager, "ABC" investment manager, in their accounts. They had the same personal representative at the same LFI. Why didn't Frank and Betty know about "ABC"?

When Frank called the advisor the next day, she stammered and paused for a moment and said, "I've been meaning to call you," and then added something about taxes. Frank never did get a clear answer, and he wondered why. When the emphasis is on marketing and acquiring new clients rather than the ongoing management of a portfolio, the advice du jour is not often distributed evenly.

My firm's experience spurred an action to broaden our view of investing and take ourselves out of the retail world of investing. Were we being sucked in to being distributors of financial products? What were others doing that we should learn from? Were we trapped into a narrow universe of investing? What might we be missing?

So, were we being sucked in to being distributors of financial products? First, there is nothing wrong or immoral about being a distributor of financial products, or of any other product for that matter. Sales and marketing is an honorable profession. That being said, the real question was: "Is what we are doing aligned with what we say we are doing?" What we said we were doing

> ### Third Horseman Clues
>
> The words and terms in the "sea of sameness" often sound like they mean the same thing. The words "fee-only" and "fee-based" are commonly confused. Learn to listen for the difference. Culture and incentives from firm to firm differ widely.

was looking out for our clients' best interests and suggesting what we would do in their situation. At the time of this introspection, we had been a fee-only firm for five years. Not fee-based, but fee-only. Fee-only means no compensation from any third-party, period. Fee-based means I will charge you a fee for advice, but I still "might" get some compensation beyond the fee. As a fee-only advisor, the thought of being a distributor and not being a trusted advisor didn't sit well. At the same time, our recommendations needed to be able to be implemented, and products/managers/ideas were part of the package in helping a client. To do that we needed to cast as wide a net as possible and do our work in evaluating and screening as objectively as possible. An outcome was that we needed to widen our scope of investment opportunities and expose ourselves to as many as possible.

What were other firms doing that we should learn from? One of the neat opportunities I've had is to be involved in our professional associations, from the local level up to the national level, with seven years on the national board of the Institute of Certified Financial Planners, including serving as the organization's president in 1998. The experience has blessed me with many friendships both nationally and internationally over the years, and has allowed me to see and discuss many excellent models under which other brilliant firms operate. At the same time, a best strength also may be a greatest weakness. Thus, was this broad and deep knowledge actually blinding our firm to what else was out there?

Turns out it was. The world of investing is made up of many of what I have come to call parallel universes. The ones I became more familiar with and that were very instructive were the family office universe and the hedge fund universe. There are others as well: the "wirehouse" universe, inhabited by the large bank/brokerage firms, and the small independent registered investment advisors universe. Although both of these had some uniqueness to their models, they were also very similar in most ways to the then-current fee-only universe we lived in.

What we learned from the hedge fund universe helped us define who we were not going to be. At the same time, new ideas and concepts that had not yet been taken to the retail level and therefore had unique advantages that had not yet been destroyed with too much money chasing became apparent. The hedge fund world provided validity to the notion that too much money chasing is a concept that ultimately changes the characteristics of the investment and most likely hinders that strategies previous usefulness in a strategy. A key point here is to fully appreciate the very common disclaimer "Past performance is no indication of future results." When a strategy that was successful goes to the "retail" marketplace, the way it performs, changes. Different ways of owning real estate is a good example. Direct ownership of income-producing real estate has been a good long-term performer. Income from rents and long-term appreciation increase somewhat over inflation with some modest leverage as well combine to give strong equity returns. Direct-owned real estate is relatively stable because it is not available for sale on a daily basis. Now put the same piece of real estate in a publicly traded real estate investment trust, and the asset has different characteristics. Because it is traded on a daily basis, the holding looks more like a stock than real estate. The old saying "If it looks like a duck, quacks like a duck, walks like a duck, and flies like a duck, it is most likely a duck" comes into play. Because it is now a liquid traded investment, it will most likely act like a stock.

The hedge fund universe understands this, and it was one of our firm's key findings. While significant due diligence and work needs to be done before investing, hedge funds should be under active consideration.

Family offices are unique organizations designed to provide a broad level of services, such as family accounting and bill paying, household and staff management, concierge-type services, and assisting a family with overall estate, philanthropy, and multigenerational communication and financial education. Of course, investing the family's wealth is the firm's key function. Family offices come in two flavors: single-family offices and multifamily offices. Because of the costs involved in running a single family office, they are often reserved for families with more than $250 million in assets. The costs of running a family office often include salaries for the executives who run many of the functions of the office, including a chief investment officer. Multifamily offices offer much the same services that single-family offices do, but the cost is spread over a number of families.

What is particularly unique about family offices is the breadth and depth of opportunities that they have access to that are never seen by most retail investors. Having the ability to write multimillion-dollar checks opens new doors that most investors and advisors are not aware of. Why? Because they are not "retail" offerings. So, the über wealthy do have access that we don't have. It turns out that money does talk. In many ways they had the same problems as generations of the family expanded and their ability to get everyone into the optimum strategies was more challenging. Not all the family members could, or should, invest at a five- or ten-million-dollar level. The answer? Pool the assets and act in the best interests of everyone. Have the process audited each year, provide consistent and accurate reporting, and provide the best advice to everyone, not just those who can afford it.

The family office model matched what everyone in the financial advisor business seemed to say and also provided the structure and opportunity to make it work. The family office model was the best to emulate, and so we did.

Were we trapped in a narrow universe of investing? Turns out in reality we were seeing and evaluating only what the retail universe had to offer. What we discovered is that you need to force yourself to be aware of what the other universes have to offer to increase your effectiveness. Investors and advisors are faced with twenty-four hours in a day and seven days a week to seek and evaluate their opportunities. Because of that it is very difficult to seek and explore other universes. Being stuck in the retail world will get you a retail outcome. By not fully exploring the investing universe, our firm was stuck with seeing what was being offered by the few firms we could follow. By opening ourselves up to experience the fullness that the multitude of investing universes had to offer, we could lower costs and enhance long-term opportunities.

Investors lose some potential by focusing too narrowly. At the same time, disciplined processes are required to avoid going snow blind in the blizzard of offerings. (Processes are covered in more detail in Chapter 9.)

CHAPTER 8

OUR OWN WORST ENEMY

The four most dangerous words in investing are "this time it's different."

—*Sir John Templeton*

Emotion in the world of portfolio investing is generally considered to be a bad thing, yet we all recognize that fear and greed are powerful motivators. Psychologists will tell us that the joy of seeing an investment's value increase is small in relation to the pain experienced when a portfolio's value declines. When the markets are down, people hesitate to invest, yet that is the best time to deploy capital. Other times when the market is down, the fear of the investments falling further becomes so overwhelming that investors feel compelled to act and sell out. "Don't worry! I'll get back in when things are more calm," they'll say. Yet they seldom get back in until the market is up, because that's when things seem to be calmer. Unfortunately, in the majority of cases this perception of safety comes at or near the peak of the market, and the cycle begins again.

Moving into retirement seems to accentuate the emotional component of investing, because at that time the investor is relying on the portfolio for the income to live out his or her hopes and dreams, and is no longer receiving a regular paycheck. A well-designed portfolio is the best way to prepare for market fluctuations. The one certainty is that the market will go up and it will go down. We would all like to know when, but although we may get lucky on occasion, we don't know. In fact, those who get "lucky" with a market call often feel pretty smart and think that market timing is their unique and special talent. Nothing could be further from the truth. Eventually, the shifting winds of the market will catch them, and the whipsawing will end up costing them a lot of their portfolio assets.

Ultimately, the question is "Why do investments perform better than investors?" That's right! Investments perform better than investors over time, due to the timing of when investors take money in and out of the market. In the chart below investor performance relative to the investments themselves is measured for the period 1984 through December 2013.

	Investor Returns[1]			Inflation	S&P 500	Barclays Aggregate Bond Index
	Equity Funds	Asset Allocation Funds	Fixed Income Funds			
Since QAIB Inception	3.69	1.85	0.70	2.80	11.11	7.67
20 Year	5.02	2.53	0.71	2.37	9.22	5.74
10 Year	5.88	2.63	0.63	2.38	7.40	4.55
5 Year	15.21	7.70	2.29	2.08	17.94	4.44
3 Year	10.87	6.26	0.70	2.07	16.18	3.27
12 Months	25.54	13.57	-3.66	1.52	32.41	-2.02

Since the inception of the study in 1984, investor returns have averaged 3.69 for equity funds versus 11.11 for the S&P 500—a spread of 7.42 percent! The different time periods of the study show that spreads tend to be different in different time periods, but tend to average 6 to 7 percent over time.

Why this is so is an important question. It turns out that investors on average make good purchase decisions 75 percent of the time, according to the study, but the 25 percent of the time they were wrong cost them a lot of money. How can that be? For the answer let's review again a chart we looked at earlier in the book:

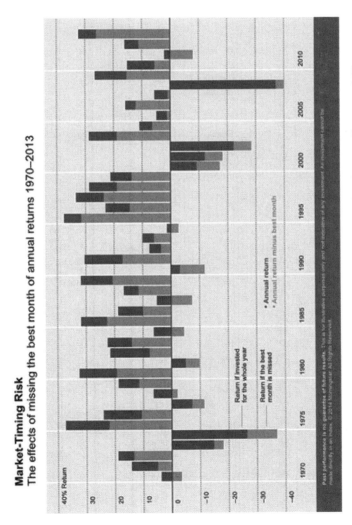

Market-Timing Risk
The effects of missing the best month of annual returns 1970–2013

@Morningstar 2014 – See Important Notice in Appendix page 162

Notice the impact of missing out on just one month of returns (the lighter portion of the bar) and the cost of missing even that short portion of the down or up period and its devastating impact to overall returns.

There are a couple of messages to accentuate here. One is that investing is not just the stock market! A properly designed and implemented portfolio will provide the best buffer for investors who need their money for both short- and long-term needs. Employing asset classes that offer true and distinct diversification will go a long way toward protecting your assets and will serve you better than moving in and out of the market. The second point is that it is important to avoid letting the daily noise of the world and markets influence your day-to-day investing efforts. The simple truth is that you do not and cannot know all the things that will come your way in investing. If the richest people in the world, including Warren Buffett, do not know, how do you expect to know? Design an all-weather strategy that will provide the protections you need.

An important part of being prepared for the unknown is having cash at the ready when the next crisis or geopolitical event comes our way. It will happen; if we knew when, planning would be so simple. But we don't! An excellent strategy is to have cash, separate from your portfolio, to use when these events occur. Well-selected and managed investments will almost always recover after a traumatic event. You just need to have the time to let the portfolio do its thing. An ample amount of cash to have on hand is eighteen to twenty-four months of living expenses if you are retired or six months if you're still receiving a paycheck of some type. Most events that affect our portfolios are reactively short term, in the twelve- to eighteen-month range. The crisis hits, time passes, things get better, and markets recover. Good portfolio design will account for that.

By separating your cash needs from your long-term investment capital allows you to use the cash, which has not declined in value, so you will not be forced to compound the cost of having an investment withdrawal. You should not consider this cash amount as part of your portfolio. The cash is the insurance policy for the short term. It is not part of your long-term investment strategy; rather, it is the short-term part of your overall financial strategy.

Occasionally, an investor likes the idea of holding cash and feels a need to have a lot of cash to balance the risk of the investment portfolio. This barbell approach is fine to a point, but too often it can be overdone. If the amount of cash exceeds the six-month guideline in the case of an employed person, or twenty-four months in the case of a retired person, some questions should be asked. For example: What about my current portfolio is so out of balance that I need this much cash? Why am I so uncomfortable with my portfolio?

Holding excess cash also limits long-term security. The investment return on cash has been consistently low, and low returns limit your ability to meet long-term goals. If you are Warren Buffet, you can afford to earn 1 percent and still live comfortably. The real question is, can you? Very few can.

Cash is your insurance policy to roll through difficult times. Its value is maximized during difficult times, and it will be vital and important to meeting current needs. It is a short-term insurance strategy. Long-term investments will carry the day to meet the goals and dreams you have for yourself and/or your loved ones.

Another challenge investors have is benchmarking their portfolios. There are a number of ways to benchmark, but in the long run, most of them have advantages and disadvantages. What better tool is there than to benchmark against your own goals? For example, if you need a 7 percent return to meet your goals and dreams, why should you care about the S&P 500? Of course, you can choose any benchmark you want, but isn't reaching your goal the most important thing?

We will discuss investment choices other than the stock market in the next chapter. If an investment choice can earn an equity-type return of 8 to 10 percent reasonably consistently with one-third the volatility of the stock market, wouldn't that be an excellent choice? Many think it would be.

Benchmarking portfolios started in the 1950s as a way for institutional investors to see how their investment managers were doing. Prior to that time, investment performance was driven more by the investor's or organization's goals, and more focus was placed on absolute returns versus the relative returns of the market. This "relative return" view may be appropriate for some investors, but my sense is that more investors would prefer more in the way of absolute returns, trading the volatile returns of relative return strategies for ones that focus more on consistency of returns. In a well-designed portfolio, the emphasis should be on both. We'll cover more on this topic in later chapters.

CHAPTER 9

ALTERNATIVE TO WHAT?

If we don't succeed, we run the risk of failure.

—*Dan Quayle*

The term "alternative investments" is used frequently in discussions about contemporary asset allocation and portfolio design. Some argue it is an asset class, yet others, like myself, see it as a broad label with a global meaning. For example, if you wanted me to describe a horse and I simply said it is a mammal, which could mean anything from a tiny field mouse to a huge whale and thousands of species in between. On the other hand, if I told you that a horse is a creature that walks and runs on four legs, is often four to six feet tall at the shoulders, has a long tail, and is used for transportation, racing, and pulling wagons, this description might at least begin to explain what a horse is and does. If you were familiar with zebras, I might be able to tell you that a horse has many of the same characteristics of a zebra, but instead of black-and-white stripes, the horse usually is one or two colors, sometimes black, and sometimes brown and white, but never in stripes. Such a description is even more robust.

Describing alternative assets as an asset class is akin to describing a horse as a mammal. Earlier in the book, the notion that investing is not limited to the stock and bond market was surfaced. Alternative assets in their various types, strategies, and configurations offer an alternative to traditional stocks and bonds. Alternative assets come in many widely differing types, each with its own unique characteristics. It is accurate to say that alternative assets are not the stock market, but some of the alternative asset categories invest in the stock market and apply various tactics and trading strategies to meet their objectives. Others are investments into commodities, real estate, venture capital, and private equity in private companies. So why are alternatives so important to contemporary portfolio design? Simply put, alternatives provide more balance to reduce volatility, so you don't have to pass up the equity-type returns that are necessary to offset inflation. You can meet your long-term objectives and reduce volatility by having assets that offer a low correlation to the traditional investment markets. (We will come back to correlations again later in this chapter.)

How can an investment reduce volatility and provide equity-type returns? Two terms come to mind: asymmetrical risk and absolute return. I would suspect that if there were an investment opportunity that would pay a 9 percent return, where the principal was stable, and it came with a US government–backed guarantee, most people would think that was a good alternative to the equity markets. After all, the long-term return for the equity markets is 9 to 10 percent, and the equity markets come with significant volatility. That is an example of an absolute return strategy. Later in this chapter, we will identify various types of strategies and their characteristics, but for now let's also explore asymmetrical risk.

Asymmetrical risk often is joined at the hip with absolute returns but deserves some additional comment. When looking at a normal distribution curve of the equity or fixed-income markets, it follows the normal bell-shaped pattern we often see, shown on page 86. It's also known as a

Gaussian model, which suggests that one standard deviation will represent two-thirds of the observations, two standard deviations will include 95 percent of the observations, and three is 99 percent of the observations. Of course, statistical measures are based on the knowledge at hand. Lately, we have heard the phrases "four or six standard deviation event" or have experienced the second hundred-year storm in the last ten years. It's important to not get too wound up in the math. Even a 1 percent chance of being incorrect presents the possibility of being totally wrong—just ask the Nobel Laureates who were the principal players in the demise of Long Term Capital Management, who nearly caused a financial meltdown in 1997. They were so convinced that the math was right that they kept doubling down and increasing the leverage of their portfolio. Their problem was that they were too concentrated (not diversified) and applied copious amounts of leverage (borrowing) to the strategy. If the leverage was not there, they would have had the time to wait. Being leveraged, they did not.

While there are always examples of very smart people who do things that end up looking not so smart, the problem is not in the math; rather, it is in relying only on the math. Risk control is a very important function in the portfolios of real people. But the math does help us better understand the opportunities that exist. If the downside risk of an investment has largely been realized, is that not a better time to invest than when the upside has been largely realized? That is the essence of asymmetrical risk return strategies. Lean the risk profile toward your advantage as an investor and have the ability to let the forces of value benefit you and your portfolio.

Let's show graphically the differences. The graph below is a representation of the stock market using a normal distribution analysis with roughly two-thirds of the observed returns in the middle of the graph and the outliers on the left and right. The negative return experiences are to the left, and the positive return experiences to the right.

Of course, the strong preference would be to experience only the right side of the graph and not the left side. As we discussed earlier, the pain of losing often exceeds the joy of gains.

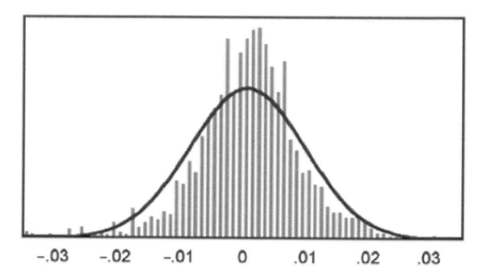

The preferred outcome is to experience what is known as a positive skew by minimizing the negative outcomes and presenting more opportunities for positive outcomes. This positive skew is an example of asymmetrical risk: less downside and more opportunity for upside. By having investments with differing characteristics than traditional investments, a portfolio can experience less volatility as a whole and bring more stability to the investing process. If an investor has a twenty-year time horizon and

Second Horseman Clues

Our knowledge base as investors needs to evolve with the changing times. As asset classes look more like one another in regard to liquidity, correlation between asset classes tends to come closer over time. Globalization has played a significant role in changing how some asset classes react and move with current events.

will have no need to invest more or withdraw capital for personal expenditures, volatility is an academic concept. Over a twenty-year time horizon, volatility for the most part doesn't matter. The portfolio has gone up and down a lot, but the timing of additions and withdrawals does not matter.

In Chapter 8, the Dalbar study showed the impact of additions and withdrawals. Some of those were deliberate timing decisions, but many were just plain "I need to make a withdrawal" for whatever the need at the moment was, whether it was income for retirement, college tuition, or another expense.

As mentioned earlier, the cost of taking withdrawals is particularly expensive during periods of market drawdowns. Ample amounts (not too much) of cash can provide the time necessary to recover capital. Yet the portfolio, if designed with some allocation to asset classes/categories exhibiting asymmetrical (more positive results likely than negative) return profiles, then those additional, diversifying characteristics will act as an additional tool to dampen volatility and thereby smoothing overall returns. If the return expectations are similar and ample liquidity is planned, these opportunities can add additional protection to a portfolio.

The nature of diversification has and is continuing to shift over time. At one point in my tenure in the advising world, it was standard practice to consider international equities as the best way to diversify a portfolio. The correlations were quite low, and you could, in fact, observe the difference in how the US and international markets reacted differently. A couple of things have changed in the past few decades. One is that the international markets are much more liquid than they used to be. Now, the international market, for the most part, is widely followed by analysts and is generally very liquid. The illiquidity premium of those markets has largely disappeared. The second thing that has happened is that the interrelated business of the world has brought correlations up to a quite high level. The diversification value has eroded considerably, but as shown in Chapter 5, when exploring asset allocation, these strategies can offer advantages to portfolios over time.

The types of strategies and tactics are quite varied, and there are many entire books dedicated to the topic, so the following is just a top-level overview of the various strategies that individually make up the alternative landscape.

Commodities

A commodity is an item that is used to satisfy a want or need. Commodities are largely considered to be fungible and considered to be as one commodity type; for example, copper is considered to be equivalent to another's supply of copper.

Active markets exist for well-established commodities, including basic resources and agricultural products. They include items such as iron ore, crude oil, coal, salt, sugar, tea, coffee beans, soybeans, aluminum, copper, rice, wheat, gold, silver, palladium, and platinum. Soft commodities are goods that are grown, while hard commodities are the ones that are extracted through mining.

Commodities are largely considered good hedges against inflation. While inflation has been low for some time, increased demand for commodities from emerging markets, including China, have kept prices relatively high.

Distressed Debt

Distressed debt refers to the securities or bonds of companies or government entities that are either already in default, under bankruptcy protection, or in distress and heading toward such a condition. Purchasing or holding such distressed debt represents significant risk, because bankruptcy may render such securities worthless (zero recovery). That being said, these securities are often acquired at very large discounts to the value of the bond or loan. The goal is very likely not to get all the way back to par value but to earn a significant return from the price at which the loan/bond was acquired.

Recently, in the community where I now live, a resort property's debt was acquired for $5 million. That gave the investors the right to foreclose on the development and acquire a property some believe to be worth $20 million. My suspicion is that their take will be less than $20 million, but a very handsome return nonetheless. The story is still being watched on how this will play out for the investors but serves as an interesting example. Clearly the skills for sourcing properties and managing real estate includes a lot of legal, valuation, and negotiation talents, but as a strategy this can be very effective.

Long/Short Equity

Long/short strategies have a lot in common with traditional equity managers in that they typically engage in a significant amount of fundamental analysis on individual companies. Where the long/short manager differs is that instead of buying only the companies he or she feels will do well, the manager will also seek out companies that may be "cruising for a bruising" and sell them short.

There are long/short managers that focus on certain industries or styles of markets. They typically attempt to reduce volatility by diversifying the positions over differing regions, market capitalization, and industry sectors.

Infrastructure Investments

The assets in an infrastructure investment tend to be toll roads, pipelines, power plants, or facilities such as hospitals. These types of investments have become popular with pension plans and large endowments. The life of the investment is very long and finite. Cash flows can be attractive on a net basis.

Some risk is present during the buildup phase with construction activities, but long-term demand is high.

Leveraged Buyouts

A form of private equity, a leveraged buyout is when a company or single asset (e.g., a real estate property) is purchased with a combination of equity and significant amounts of borrowed money, structured in such a way that the target's cash flows or assets are used as the collateral (or "leverage") to secure and repay the money borrowed to purchase the target company/asset.

Mezzanine Debt

This is a form of private equity in which a hybrid debt issue is subordinated to another debt issue from the same issuer. Mezzanine debt has embedded equity instruments (usually warrants) attached, which increase the value of the subordinated debt and allow for greater flexibility when dealing with bondholders. Mezzanine debt is frequently associated with acquisitions and buyouts, where it may be used to prioritize new owners ahead of existing owners in case of bankruptcy.

Real Estate

Many consider the ownership of a home to be a form of real estate equity, but in this sense, it is purely real estate held for investment purposes and not personal use. Forms can be in residential rental properties, such as apartments or office/warehouse properties. Raw land and farm land are other possibilities.

The use of loans/leverage is a common way to enhance the returns on rental real estate. While property does tend to appreciate faster than inflation, it is only slightly so. The business operations that call for increased rents account for more of the returns. Typically, nearly 75 percent of the returns from real estate come from the rental income.

Timberland

While timberland in one sense is real estate, it has very different characteristics. The returns on these forestland investments come from biological growth, upward product class movement, timber price appreciation, and land price appreciation.

The benefits of timberland investments arise from the tendency for the investments to be negatively correlated with other investment instruments, such as stocks and bonds. This negative correlation allows timberlands to be used to diversify a portfolio. Timberland investments also provide relatively high returns for the low risk they carry.

However, timberland investments are not perfect investments; they are still open to risks such as high purchase prices that can depress returns, natural disasters that can destroy the forestland underlying the investment, and price risks associated with the price of the trees on the land.

Venture Capital

Venture capital (VC) is financial capital provided to early stage, high potential growth startup companies. The venture capital fund earns money by owning equity in the companies it invests in, which usually have a novel technology or business model in high-technology industries, such as biotechnology, IT, and software. The typical venture capital investment occurs after the seed-funding round, as the first round of institutional capital to fund growth (also referred to as the Series A round) in the interest of generating a return through an eventual realization event, such as an IPO or trade sale of the company. Venture capital is a type of private equity.

In addition to angel investing and other seed-funding options, venture capital is attractive for new companies with limited operating history that are too small to raise capital in the public markets and have not reached the point where they are able to secure a bank loan or complete a debt offering. In exchange for the high risk venture capitalists assume by investing in smaller and less-mature companies, they usually get significant control over company decisions, in addition to a significant portion of the company's ownership (and consequently, value).

Structured Products

Structured products are designed to facilitate highly customized risk-return objectives. This is accomplished by taking a traditional security, such as a conventional investment-grade bond, and replacing the usual payment features (e.g., periodic coupons and final principal) with nontraditional payoffs derived not from the issuer's own cash flow, but from the performance of one or more underlying assets.

The payoffs from these performance outcomes are contingent in the sense that if the underlying assets return "x," then the structured product pays out "y." This means that structured products closely relate to traditional models of option pricing, though they may also contain other derivative types, such as swaps, forwards, and futures, as well as embedded features, such as leveraged upside participation or downside buffers.

The complexity of derivative securities has long kept them out of meaningful representation in traditional retail (and many institutional) investment portfolios. Structured products can bring many of the benefits of derivatives to investors who otherwise would not have access to them. As a complement to more traditional investment vehicles, structured products have a useful role to play in modern portfolio management.[11]

The Alternative Challenge

So you may be saying to yourself, that's cool! If I can get an equity-type return with less volatility, why wouldn't I put all my assets in alternatives? In the case of the Yale Endowment, mentioned in Chapter 4, well over 50 percent of the portfolio is in various alternative strategies. If you are confident that your need for liquidity from the portfolio will not exceed the income generated from the investments, then the attractiveness of alternatives rises a few notches. Most investors have issues with not being able to get at least a portion of their portfolio immediately, and in the alternative world, that just isn't an option. In the case of the large endowments, they are generally mandated not to use principal, but distribute a percentage of assets for the endowment's stated purposes, typically 5 percent.

There almost always are provisions in the documents for alternative investments speaking to the availability to funds. Terms such as "lock-up" and "notice requirements" need to be understood and recognized as being different from investing in a stock or traditional mutual fund. The reason for these provisions isn't simply to put a barrier between you and your money. These strategies usually take some time to play out, and consequently the manager of the strategy wants to have time to unwind a particular tactic or strategy to protect *all* the investors in the fund.

During the Great Recession, some funds exercised their rights to stop withdrawals, a practice commonly called "gates." Of course, investors

---

[11] investopidia.com and wikipedia.com were used as resources for the various alternative asset descriptions.

often immediately jump to the conclusion that this practice is solely in the manager's interests, and in some cases that could be true. Yet, it could also be true that the sophisticated strategies employed in carrying out the objectives need time to develop in a prudent and reasonable manner.

So alternatives may be an important part of the portfolio, but having 100 percent alternatives tips the scale from reducing volatility to locking up capital to an extent that may not be advisable.

Another reason some alternative strategies can deliver higher returns is their ability to invest in illiquid investments. In Chapter 6 we discussed the building block method of estimating investment returns. Conceptually we can expand on the concept and suggest that the levels of additional return are based on the investor taking higher. Illiquidity is one form of that risk. We already discussed that international and small cap stocks, because they are less liquid, experienced higher overall returns since investors as a group did not pay as high a price for those securities based on the increased risk. We also explored the notion that as asset classes became more liquid, they became more highly correlated with one another, and the spread of returns lessened.

So it is not a huge leap to understand that the illiquidity of an asset class deserves and receives compensation through higher returns for the increased illiquidity risk assumed. This illiquidity is present in many forms of alternative assets, including venture capital, leveraged buyouts, and real estate. The increased nominal returns are reasonable. The question for investors is how much illiquidity is reasonable in their current circumstances.

Eric and Fran loved their alternatives. They were enjoying a nice high single-digit to low double-digit cash flow from their investments. They thought, "We don't need liquidity; our income fulfills all our needs." Suddenly and unexpectedly, they needed to raise $250,000 to help their son and daughter-in-law out of a jam. If their son didn't get the money soon, he and his wife and their two young children would be out on the street. Most of Eric and Fran's investments were in non-traded REITs. Cash flow was being paid, but the bank wouldn't use them as collateral, so they started looking for a buyer. Then, one day a letter came from a firm offering to buy shares in one of the REITs—for 50 percent of what Eric and Fran had paid! Due to the urgency of the situation, they accepted the offer.

Which side of the transaction would you prefer to be on? Eric and Fran's, or the purchaser of the asset for fifty cents on the dollar who was paying for a strong cash yield? As this example illustrates, keeping some liquidity is advisable.

A lot of mutual fund companies now offer new funds under the term "alternatives." A few questions come to mind. If a fund is promising daily liquidity, can the fund actually in fact invest in less than liquid investments? How does the investment dynamic change when you need to have the ability to raise cash on any given day? For some strategies, such as long/short equity and managed futures, the difference is most likely minimal because the underlying assets are liquid, daily-traded securities. For other strategies, such as real estate (not REITs), the funds are holding lots of cash to meet the objective. Our view is that you would be better off holding your own cash than paying fund managers a fee to hold your cash.

CHAPTER 10

GLOBAL DISRUPTIONS AND DISLOCATIONS

You can't solve a problem with the same mind that created it.

—Albert Einstein

You probably have been noticing that the fourth horseman has not gotten much attention. There are a couple of reasons for the delay: 1) The fourth horseman presents a constantly shifting landscape and needs to be dealt with separately, and 2) the fourth horseman in many ways fuels the impact of the other three horsemen. The fourth horseman should be considered the captain of the four-horseman team. As captain, the fourth horseman creates events and circumstances that cheer on the second horseman, volatility, with new and sometimes shocking events that investors react to, sometimes inappropriately. The changes the fourth horseman delivers change the supply and demand expectations, which result in the change in prices of goods and services. The third horseman, "the sea of sameness," lulls investors into a false sense of confidence, leaving them unprepared and vulnerable to the other three horsemen. The fourth horseman knows that change is inevitable, and not paying attention to his work will have lower-than-desired results.

There are two dramatic forces that the fourth horseman brings to the fight that have negative impacts on portfolios. The first is the emergence of shocking geopolitical events, and the second is the change that occurs as a result of emerging technologies and changes to our way of life. Too often investors focus on geopolitical events as the issue. Yes, it is true that events of a geopolitical nature have an impact on the investment markets, most often with a short-term burst of volatility. On page 98 is a chart from Ned Davis Research and you can see the impact on the S&P 500 immediately following such an event. In some cases it is clear that the event had no impact, or the impact lasted for only a short period of time. Let's examine the weapons of the fourth horseman and the havoc they wreak on investor's portfolios.

The fourth horseman is not exclusively about these "events." The fourth horseman is more insidious and has a greater impact than a single occurrence of strife. The fourth horseman's global displacements and transformations are often the cause of the events that serve as a crescendo to the change the fourth horseman placed on a country or society. The availability, or lack thereof, of a resource critical to people's needs (or perceived as such) can often be pointed to as a reason to "rise up."

Global displacements and transformations have occurred since the beginning of time. One can start with our prehistoric ancestors and their ability to harness the use of fire for preparing food and providing comfort. Of course, the use of the wheel was a biggie, too. With the wheel, large objects could be transported that were impossible to transport before. Consider how impossible the pyramids would be to build if the wheel didn't exist. New disruptive ideas and tools build upon each

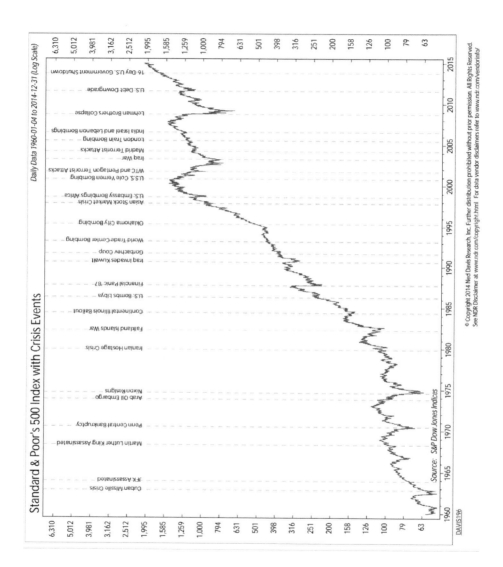

Standard & Poor's 500 Index with Crisis Events

Daily Data 1960-01-04 to 2014-12-31 (Log Scale)

Source: S&P Dow Jones Indices

DAVIS196

other. There have been many other transformational events in history. Events such as the Gutenberg press, which revolutionized the way information was distributed to the masses. Many pieces of the printing press had already been in existence, but the innovation of metal movable type increased the production capability dramatically.

If this book were a history book, I could recount thousands of innovations that changed the world, such as the steam engine, mass production lines, electrical lighting, and on and on and on. The fourth horseman is not a history lesson per se, but rather a recognition that change has always been with us, and it brings us to the human race's best talent: pattern recognition.

Since prehistoric times a human's survival has been based on the ability to recognize danger. One needs to see the outcome of an encounter with a saber-toothed tiger only once to trigger the brain's immediate reaction. You will quickly recognize that touching a flame induces pain and should be avoided.

Most of the big changes in history changed life slowly and deliberately. In most cases, the impact of the "revolutionary" idea happened over a long period of time as people came to recognize that the "new way" was in fact better than what they were accustomed to. Certain artisans hold on to the old ideas as some romantic notion of keeping in touch with an earlier time, but there is no ability to scale the old ideas in comparison to the new innovations. It just isn't possible. Printing pages one at a time with historic presses still happens, but the practice severely limits the amount of knowledge and wisdom that can be shared. The oft-used analogy of the buggy whip manufacturer's experience after the use of the automobile went mainstream is appropriate. Somebody still manufactures buggy whips, but a growth industry it is not.

Let's fast-forward to our current environment. The pace of change and the new realities that it brings have accelerated dramatically. Today a person can be his or her own publisher and newsroom. A report about an event can be instantaneous and can have immediate distribution globally at little or no cost. The recent events geopolitically—including but not limited to the "Arab Spring"—were driven by the ability to distribute information quickly and engage a large audience. Not tomorrow, not next week, but immediately! This change has come at us humans very quickly, with little luxury to adapt to new patterns in our best tool, pattern recognition, which in turn creates a sense of uncertainty and fear. The oft-quoted "Moore's Law" indicates that the capability of computer chips doubles roughly every two years. Today the average smartphone has more computing capacity than was available in the large mainframe computers used to put a man on the moon in 1969. Fifty years ago, it was a big deal to make a long-distance phone call across the United States; it was expensive and reserved for important occasions. Today we can call someone in India or on the African continent, and cost is of little concern. Putting cost aside, the mere *ability* to communicate on this scale is amazing. The technological advances have increased our access to information and have changed the way we interact with other humans and how we live our day to day lives.

There is little question that the world is more connected and the cost of communication continues to drop. Most of us in 2014 can access e-mail, do web research, shop, and perform dozens of other tasks via mobile devices. The results of my entire medical exam, including tests like EKGs, are available on my tablet and cell phone.

So how is this relevant to investing? In spite of all the evidence that emotions are contraindicated to smart investing, fear and greed are the dominant drivers of investment decision-making. As pointed out in the Dalbar study in Chapter 7, people invest and invest more when they feel good and tend to invest less or to withdraw capital when they are concerned and afraid. The pace of change has changed dramatically, challenging the pattern-recognition capability of the normal human investor, who has not adapted. The "frames" investors create in which to conduct their evaluations may or may not still be relevant. If your evaluation system is still designed for buggy whip manufacturers or saber-toothed tigers, the outcome will not be consistent with the objectives sought to meet your goals and dreams.

Continued technological advances are the catalysts of dislocations and transformations in many areas including:

1. **Geopolitics**. The best way to control a large group of people is to control the information they can receive. If an alternative to the current state of existence is not available for comparison, the current state of affairs may seem acceptable. The proliferation of mobile communication devices hinders the ability to control information and empowers people via their ability to communicate. While we in the United States have relatively open access to information, this is not as true across the globe. Yet even in environments that are more restrictive, the population in most countries across the globe have a significantly increased ability to communicate and interact with one another. These "interactions" empower people to take actions that were not possible a few decades ago.

2. **Life and lifestyles**. Consider just a few of the changes and new opportunities that have been made available in the past few years. Uber, which started as a freaky alternative to taxis, is now catching regulators' eyes due to its success. Airbnb is a viable alternative to expensive hotel rooms. Facebook, Twitter, LinkedIn, and other social media sites have multibillion-dollar market caps because they can create communities and serve as a medium to distribute marketing messages.

3. **Financial services.** Accessibility to data has never been easier. Transferring money between accounts can be accomplished with a smartphone on a 24/7 basis. Orders for the purchase or

sale of securities can be accomplished in the same way. Banks are leaving the small business lending space, and the void is being filled by web-based lending organizations. This is just the beginning. Such realities will increase accessibility, reduce costs, and create new and different opportunities.

4. **Health care.** With little question, the nature and shape of the delivery of health care is undergoing massive and impactful change. The Affordable Care Act is just one major catalyst. An aging population will bring increasingly difficult challenges as the percentage of individuals age sixty-five or older becomes a higher percentage of the population. New technologies can both help and present new difficulties. Each new advance that allows people to live longer will be met by challenges that more people "of a certain age" encounter.

Investors need to find ways to appreciate the new dynamics of investing yet be cognizant of the notion that, just because it is new, it isn't necessarily the "next greatest thing." Also worth considering is that many new ideas go through many hits and misses in the early stages of their existence. Looking back at the early starts of Google, Microsoft, and Apple, we can observe that although they clearly became the "next greatest thing," that wasn't always the case.

For a defense against the fourth horseman, broad-based diversification and allocations to investments that exhibit asymmetrical risk profiles are critical. History has proven that a focus on "the new way of doing things" often leads to bad outcomes. Some will make it; some won't. To ignore or pooh-pooh that new idea is also silly. Too many "grandpa" portfolios full of ideas that worked in the 1950s and 1960s exist. Portfolios that have a probability of success will provide a defense against the shifts that the fourth horseman will inevitably bring about.

CHAPTER 11

THE OVERALL PORTFOLIO

The nice thing about doing a crossword puzzle is,
you know there is a solution.

—Stephen Sondheim

There is an answer to every investment design puzzle as well, but there will always be some leftover puzzle pieces, because not all the pieces may be appropriate for each individual situation. Differing objectives are like a puzzle that creates a different picture depending on how it gets put together. In the last chapter, the case was made that alternatives can have lower volatility and equity like returns. Earlier in the book, the case for the endowment model was made, with the understanding that the large endowments do not have the same need for liquidity as individuals. The siren song for alternatives has been recognized by many large endowments, and several have allocated well over 50 percent to alternative investments. Yet how this all applies to individual investors is an important question. On one hand lower volatility and equity-type returns are attractive. At the same time, flexibility for unknown events is important and liquidity is a prime concern.

Too many investors think they need to go "all in" on an idea, concept, or strategy. After all, doesn't this make the most sense based on what I know, just learned, or believe? Yes, we must believe in what we are doing, yet being too dogmatic can increase risk or dampen opportunities. The "great debate" referenced earlier regarding different investing styles can be an interesting discussion. At the same time deciding whether to invest in a passive or index strategy as opposed to an active strategy doesn't help us answer the real question. "How can I meet my long-term goals and objectives? Isn't what's important meeting the goals and objectives? In many ways the debate about passive and active investing gets in the way of moving forward in a positive manner. Like most everything else in life, the answer is not at the extremes of a debate but somewhere in the wonderful middle.

> **Four Horsemen Clues**
>
> A portfolio must defend against all four horsemen. No one idea will carry the day in the long term. A mixture of ideas and concepts into an overall portfolio with built-in defenders against each horseman is required.

Why force a choice at all? In some cases the passive choice is appropriate, and in other cases the active approach makes more sense. Well, guess what? The passive index fund and the actively managed fund will not care in the least if they are sitting next to each other in a portfolio. They will coexist quite happily. Earlier in the book, we discovered that highly liquid and well-followed markets are more difficult for a manager to add value and that less liquid assets provided more opportunity to discover hidden value and exceed the returns an index provides. The highly liquid asset classes like US stock and developed international may be a place to consider a passive strategy. If an investor chooses not to go through the effort or does not find a reasonable choice, the passive fund is a choice that is reasonable and will do what it is expected to do. There are cases, however, where managers can and do add value. Following a process like the one outlined in the following chapter can help ferret out appropriate choices.

In most cases a balanced approach, sometimes known as the core and satellite allocation approach, makes the most sense. In this approach a significant allocation is invested in traditional investment vehicles, such as stocks and bonds in either their individual form or in mutual funds or ETFs. The core portfolio is designed to have some flexibility/liquidity via more liquid investment choices and still allow for a meaningful allocation to strategies that will likely reduce volatility and produce reasonable returns. Individual circumstances, desires for a certain level of return, and expected levels of volatility within individual parameters are important factors to consider in the design of an overall portfolio.

Using data such as expected returns, covariances, and standard deviations; we can ascertain the likely outcomes of this portfolio mix.

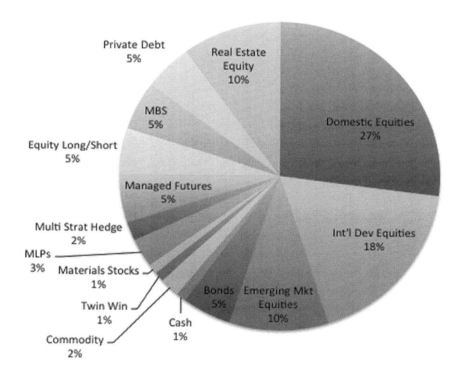

For example, an investor decides to allocate 30 percent of his portfolio to several alternative strategies, and the balance of 70 percent to an allocation of stock and fixed income. The pie chart on the previous page shows one such allocation. This approach has a number of different types of investments, which offer various expectations for returns and volatility.

The next table shows the assumptions being employed. Reasonable people will differ on the return assumptions used. This is normal and to be expected. As you might expect, assumptions such as these are snapshots of a moment in time and are not likely to persist. For this reason we caution that these are for illustrative purposes and should not be relied upon for personal use. Professional advice and/or your own hard work should be the source of any assumptions used for your personal portfolio design.

			Annualized Mean	Ann. Standard Deviation
Domestic Equities			8.0%	16.0%
Int'l. Dev. Equities			9.0%	17.0%
Emerging Mkt. Equities			10.0%	24.0%
Bonds			2.5%	3.0%
Cash			0.1%	0.1%
Commodities			5.0%	12.0%
Twin Win			7.0%	13.0%
Materials Stocks			8.0%	20.0%
MLPs			15.0%	16.0%
Multistrategy Hedge			15.0%	10.0%
Managed Futures			5.0%	12.0%
Equity Long/Short			13.0%	9.0%
MBS			4.0%	3.0%
Private Debt			9.0%	2.0%
Real Estate Equity			12.0%	5.0%

The chart on page 109 is laid out with volatility being measured as standard deviation on the bottom or horizontal axis, and return on the left or vertical axis. The farther to the right, the higher the expected volatility. Often, the higher the volatility, the higher the rate of expected return. However, the combination of certain assets classes can reduce the volatility. The square farthest to the right is representative of the S&P 500 of 100 percent equities, and the square to the left of it is representative of the risk-return trade-offs (see assumptions and important notes on page 161) of the 70 percent allocated to traditional investments and the 30 percent allocated to alternatives. Note the significant reduction of the level of risk with little sacrifice of return.

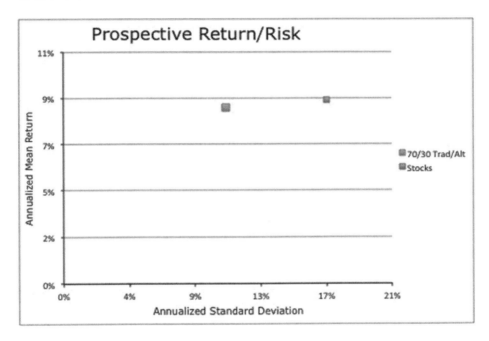

This reduction in volatility is important for real portfolios being relied upon by real people. As we discussed earlier, the costs of using capital when the portfolio values are down presents a double whammy on the portfolio. As investors we have much more control over risk than we do return.

As a further example, let's increase the percentage of alternatives and see how the results can change: further reductions in volatility and no sacrifice in expected returns. It is clear why the large endowments have gone in this direction. The trade-off is giving up some of the "make-up" years of very high returns in liquid public equities for a more stable return stream. This is much like taking a trip in which you can choose a road with many twists and turns and bumps along the way, or a smooth and straight highway. Occasionally, I like the twists and turns, as I'm a bit of a car nut. But most often, like most people, I prefer the smooth, straight, and comfortable way to my destination. Contemporary portfolio design is more like the latter than the former.

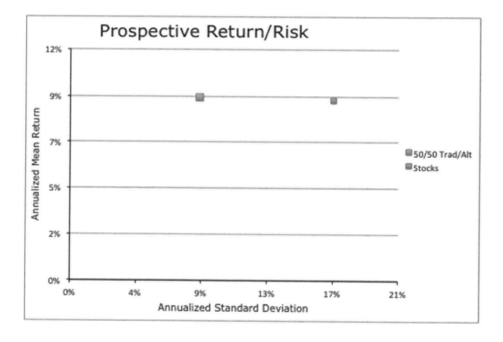

Using a core and satellite strategy allows an investor to have multiple opportunities and, ultimately, a portfolio that can "roll with the punches" as different economic events come along. Remember, there are no market timers on the list of great investors. Having investments that work together well will not give an investor the highest return in any one year, but it does offer the highest probability of long-term investment success.

Care has been made to not provide a pat answer to what is often heard in the marketplace about "no-lose investments" where the "sky is the limit." Logically, we all know where these ideas will end up based on our own experiences. A high-probability investment strategy is based on the recognition that we don't and can't know all that will happen. We do know that the investment of capital is largely driven by the emotions of fear and greed. We also know that if the portfolio is designed well with investments that behave differently from one another, then the portfolio can mitigate potential damage and present opportunities during good times.

CHAPTER 12

MANAGER SELECTION

*If you pick the right people and give them the op-
portunity to spread their wings—and put compensation as a carrier behind it—you almost don't
have to manage them.*

—Jack Welch

Let's make a couple of assumptions for this chapter. One is that a
decision has been made to employ a multi-asset multi-manager
approach for implementing a portfolio. As mentioned earlier, if the
decision is made to use a passive, or index approach, the process really
comes down to assessing how much tracking error may be associated
with a particular fund relative to its index. Tracking error is the amount
of variance a fund has to the index. For example, if the S&P 500 index
is up 10 percent and the index fund is up 9.5 percent, then there is a
negative tracking error of 0.5 percent, and if the numbers were reversed,
with the manager being up 10 percent and the index being up only 9.5
percent, the 0.5 percent becomes a positive tracking error. Clearly, if

you want to index, you want the tracking error to be as small as possible. This can be found on the funds information page published by the fund company. It's either stated explicitly or easy to calculate. One of the factors to account for in evaluating the tracking error is the fees. There are significant variances between index funds on fees, and an examination of the fee level is important.

If one has decided to allocate exclusively to index funds, and the tracking error and fees are compared between alternate funds in a particular asset class, then a majority of the work is complete.

The other path is to consider the active path for manager selection. This will require a process to identify the managers who are consistently ranked in the top 20 percent of their category. This will require the work to go much deeper and wider than necessary for index funds. This may be enough for many to say, "I'll take the easier path," because the additional work and costs of data are not worth it to them. There always needs to be a payoff when additional effort and costs are involved. An additional 1 percent over time is a significant sum. Let's take a look at the return on one million dollars at 8, 9, and 10 percent over ten-, fifteen-, twenty-, and thirty-year time frames:

Number of Years	8%	9%	10%
10	$2,158,925	$2,367,363	$2,593,742
15	$3,172,169	$3,642,482	$4,177,248
20	$4,660,957	$5,604,410	$6,727,499
30	$10,062,656	$13,267,678	$17,449,402

Even relatively small incremental increases in returns add up to significant sums. Of course, all this needs to be done net of the additional fees that active management will incur. Otherwise, what is the point? Can consistent managers be found? We believe that with some work and a good process, the answer is yes. Of course, not all managers will out-perform all the time, but identifying the 20 percent that do is about research, evaluation, and solid due diligence. The same process that is used to hire and engage managers needs to be used to fire managers when appropriate. (More on that later in this chapter.)

Many investors have had less than satisfying outcomes when relying on sales representatives and brokers to provide them with the results of their firm's wonderful research. There are many reasons for this, includ-ing the involvement of the "compensation committee" as we explored in Chapter 7. The Large Financial Institution (LFI) expects to get paid and will seek to extract a pound of flesh from the managers. Of course, the LFIs should get paid for the services they provide, but if they exclude managers solely based on compensation? Maybe, not so cool! We refer to this part of the process as the "compensation committee." Experience has shown that casting a very wide net and using a consistent and dis-ciplined process for evaluating funds and managers by using objective data, the top managers will become apparent. Soon you will have a short list to dig into more deeply through a consistent, disciplined process. A key question to ask of or about an advisor is what process he or she uses in evaluating and choosing investments or investment managers. If the answer refers to the firm's wonderful research and lists of managers, then the "compensation committee" may in fact be in charge. On the other hand, if the answer focuses on the process—how the information is gathered and evaluated and put into place—those are clues that the advisor is intimately familiar with the process, understands what the pro-cess is designed to do, and is acting as more than the salesperson parrot-ing company marketing lines.

Of course, no one person can "know" all the managers and strategies, because they number in the tens of thousands. This reality, combined with hundreds of data points for each manager, can make the research process seem overwhelming and impossible to do well. The good news is there are a multitude of providers that provide access to tools where screening can be used to sift through the sea of data to create manageable lists.

Some of these data providers include:

- Morningstar

- PSN (offered by Informa Information Systems)

- Prequin

- Barclay Hedge

- Eureka Hedge

- Hedge Fund Research

- Morgan Hedge

- Hedge Fund Intelligence

- Credit Suisse (hedgeindex.com)

These are searchable databases with multiple managers in the mutual fund, exchange-traded fund (ETF), managed account, and hedge fund space. A couple will provide some information on real estate managers as well. Other interesting sources for real estate include the National Council of Real Estate Professional Fiduciaries (NCREIF.org) and the Stanger Report. NCREIF has a number of databases an investor can subscribe to in which the real estate is broken down into various categories such as residential (apartments), industrial, office, and so on. The Stanger Report has a long history of tracking and monitoring real estate limited partnerships and nontraded real estate investment trusts

(REITs). Stanger evaluates new partnerships and REITs coming to market and their deal terms, which is very helpful in comparing various offerings. Of course, there are others, but those provided here are the most significant.

The larger the database is and the fewer the conflicts of interest, the better. The databases are varied as to how many managers are followed and the number of data points they include. You will find out very quickly that there is a lot of free data; however, it is often very surface oriented, simply providing return data for various periods. Those seeking superior management will likely find the free information insufficient. The elegance of these programs/databases is that they allow an investor to sort a number of criteria. The free versions allow for few data points and offer little in the way of evaluation. The paid versions will offer hundreds of data fields, including some statistical measures, such as total return for various periods, maximum drawdown of capital for any one period, and year-to-date returns. For example, say you want to focus on the up capture, or the amount a manager or group of managers returned during certain market events. These results can be compared to the Dow Jones Industrial Average, S&P 500, or a variety of fixed-income and hedge fund indexes for comparison.

> **Things to do and watch for...**
>
> - Do examine multiple time series.
>
> - Watch for large "outsized" returns in one or two years.
>
> - Focus on consistency, not end-of-period results.

As a firm we like to see return and alpha data over multiple time periods. It is common to see a manager have a wonderful performance over one or two years, especially early in a strategy's beginning. There are a couple of reasons for this. One is that during a fund's early stages, the challenge is to add capital. As a fund ages, the need to deal with capital withdrawals brings a new set of requirements to the process. Month to month, or quarter to quarter, the amount of invested capital will fluctuate in many strategies. In the early stages, the manager is focused on what to buy, and later on the focus could be at times on what he or she needs to sell and whether or not doing so is appropriate. A second reason early performance may not be sustainable is that with beginning capital amounts, the amount of ideas the manager can deploy is limited to smaller amounts of capital. This forces the manager to pick the absolute best ideas. Why can't the manager continue this focus? It is possible the manager can't because all the money that can go to that idea (or those ideas) has been deployed. Larger funds' returns tend to diminish on a relative basis as the fund gets larger. The absolute best ideas are added to the really, really good ideas, and then the really good ideas, and so on.

You may have gotten the impression that researching alternatives can be complicated and expensive, and for the most part it is. There are services that offer "due diligence reports" on managers, and they will run $3,000 and up for a full dossier on a particular strategy. The due diligence questionnaire we use is included in the appendix. Although the questionnaire will need to be modified to meet an investor's individual needs, it is nevertheless a good place to start.

The following few paragraphs explain some of the more important measurements our firm pays attention to when evaluating a manager or strategy. These various measurements all shed light on the pieces of the investment puzzle and show how each piece will interact with other pieces of the portfolio.

Short-term performance provides clues, but weaker ones than we like for assessing consistency and superiority. For that reason, looking at annual returns for up to ten years is important. Unusually large excess returns in any one or two years should be evaluated skeptically. Keep in mind that a huge outlier return in any particular year brings the average return up. But consider why that return occurred and whether it is repeatable through the manager's skill. One of the things you are looking for in an alternative strategy is the consistency of the returns over time.

Another data point we pay particular attention to is called alpha. Alpha is defined as a measure of performance on a risk-adjusted basis. Alpha takes the volatility (price risk) of a mutual fund and compares its risk-adjusted performance to a benchmark index. In other words, it is the excess return of the fund relative to the return of the benchmark index. Using a relevant benchmark to compare is important, as volatility is a key component in the calculation. Looking at the one-, three-, five-, seven-, and ten-year alphas, assuming the data is available, can give a sense of the consistency of returns and what management has brought to the table in terms of skill.

Up capture and down capture statistics will also provide valuable information on manager skill. A base number for up and down capture is 100. An up capture statistic of 100 means the manager's return in his or her strategy was exactly equal to the relevant benchmark. An up capture of 120 means the strategy outperformed the benchmark by 20 percent. For example, if the benchmark was up 10 percent and the up capture statistic was 120, then the manager's strategy provided a 12 percent return, 2 percent being 20 percent of the benchmark return. Down capture shows what happens in a down market. If the relevant benchmark showed a drawdown in capital of 5 percent and the manager's strategy was down 6 percent, the down capture is also 120. This time, though, the 120 number is a negative, not a positive, as the loss exceeded the

> **Things to do or watch for...**
>
> Up and down capture statistics can be very instructive in evaluating managers. Be sure to match them against relative benchmarks. Not all managers should be compared to the S&P 500.

benchmark. What the investor is seeking is a strategy that exhibits better than 100 for the up capture and less than 100 for the down capture. This combination shows a more relative up-rise and less relative downside for a particular strategy.

Other statistical measures such as R2, Sortino, and Sharpe ratios can also provide important statistics to show how a strategy has performed on a relative basis and how consistent the manager's skill has been.

The Sharpe ratio tells us whether a portfolio's returns are due to smart investment decisions or a result of excess risk. Although one portfolio or fund can reap higher returns than its peers, it is only a good investment if those higher returns do not come with too much additional risk. The greater a portfolio's Sharpe ratio, the better its risk-adjusted performance has been. A negative Sharpe ratio indicates that a riskless asset would perform better than the security being analyzed.[12]

The Sortino ratio's formula does not penalize a portfolio manager for volatility and instead focuses on whether returns are negative or below a certain threshold. The mean in the Sortino ratio formula represents the returns a portfolio manager is able to get above the return that an investor expects.

A modification of the Sharpe ratio differentiates harmful volatility from general volatility by taking into account the standard deviation of negative asset returns, called downside deviation. The Sortino ratio subtracts the risk-free rate of return from the portfolio's return, and then divides that by the downside deviation. A large Sortino ratio indicates a low probability of a large loss.

Sortino Ratio

Determining whether to use the Sharpe ratio or Sortino ratio depends on whether you want to focus on standard deviation or downside deviation.

---

[12] Sharpe, Sortino, and R2 definitions from investopedia.com.

Sharpe ratios are better at analyzing portfolios that have low volatility because the Sortino ratio won't have enough data points to calculate downside deviation. This makes the Sortino ratio better when analyzing highly volatile portfolios.

Assuming you have gotten to a short list of alternative managers, the next step is to complete the due diligence process by asking the right questions and validating the information you have found. Rather than duplicate information, I will refer again to the due diligence question-naire in the appendix of this book regarding what questions to ask and the data to look for.

Still another way to access alternatives is the many new offerings in mutual funds. Using liquid mutual funds, ETFs, and asset class–specific index funds can provide a measure of replication of index values. As mentioned earlier in this chapter, there is an open question as to how one can convert an illiquid strategy into a liquid one and still enjoy the low correlations the asset class enjoyed while in its native state. As is often said, "nothing is impossible," yet it seems logical that if you change the asset itself, expecting similar results may seem to be a stretch. As of the writing of this book, these offerings are still very new. We remain skeptical but are keeping a watchful eye. The liquid alternative offerings do offer lower investment minimums and much greater access. Will this lead to too much of a good thing? It is yet to be determined.

R-squared is a statistical measure that represents the percentage of a fund or security's movements that can be explained by movements in a benchmark index. For fixed-income securities, the benchmark is the T-bill. For equities, the benchmark is often the S&P 500.

R-squared values range from 0 to 100. An R-squared of 100 means that all movements of a security are completely explained by movements in the index. A high R-squared (between 85 and 100) indicates the fund's performance patterns have been in line with the index. A fund with a low R-squared (70 or less) doesn't act much like the index.

A higher R-squared value will indicate a more useful beta figure. For example, if a fund has an R-squared value of close to 100 but has a beta below 1, it is most likely offering higher risk-adjusted returns. A low R-squared means you should ignore the beta.

All of these statistical measures are tools to evaluate a manager's skill, one versus another. If a manager is going to engage in active management, the skill is what you are paying for, and these tools provide methods to assess the relative merits of each. When using these tools, however, be sure that the benchmarks are indeed relevant and have like characteristics. Comparing a fixed-income strategy to the S&P 500 may be interesting, but in the end is not very instructive. As mentioned earlier, benchmark data is available through a variety of sources.

The measures described are indicators of the relative performance of a manager or strategy to an index. If the index proves to be the better choice, so be it. The burden of proof is on the active strategy, not the index.

In researching databases you will find out very quickly that this data is not inexpensive. Access to quality reports start in the few thousand dollar range and can run into the tens of thousands, which may be prohibitive for smaller investors. One choice is to use an advisor who does use tools such as these and can demonstrate the knowledge and ability to use them for the benefit of clients. The process and measurements themselves can be incorporated into questions to ask advisors about the process and tools they use. Chapter 13 and the appendix provide tools for selecting and monitoring investment managers. In chapter 14 we will explore more about finding, interviewing, and engaging advisors. Clearly, engaging with someone who can spread the costs of these tools over several clients has its advantages. Yet more important is finding an advisor who can articulate knowledge of sound screening and selection tools and demonstrate that he or she does not just rely on a "research department."

CHAPTER 13

MONITORING AND ONGOING ASSESSMENT

Diligence is the mother of good luck.

—*Benjamin Franklin*

The harder I work the luckier I get.

—*Thomas Jefferson*

Portfolio management is work. Consistent work and effort is rewarded in the long term. As I review portfolios for new potential clients, I will often find two types of portfolios. One type is what one popular financial magazine or another might tout. The cover would have said something like "The Top Ten (fill in the blank with stocks, mutual funds, bonds, etc.) to Own Now." Of course, this compelling headline was most likely based on a listing based on recent past performance, and the performance lagged over time because it was not reviewed, or the methodology to create this list was no longer relevant.

The second type of portfolio is one where the investor did use many of the principles outlined in previous chapters and came up with a portfolio that fit his or her unique circumstances. For a while this portfolio did meet expectations because of the sound process followed, but because the process was in effect "put on the shelf," the portfolio's relevance waned over time as client objectives and needs changed and the circumstances and market expectations used in the original selection work also changed. Of course, there are those who do establish a sound process and review it continuously. We seldom see these individuals because they love working on their portfolio, follow sound principles, and do the work themselves. On the rare occasions when we do meet with an individual in this camp, we are quick to point out that he or she really doesn't need us. A few engage us anyway, because they want a manager for their spouse or other loved one and want the process to extend beyond their influence. In any case, we have proved consistently that by following good process, portfolios tend to stay relevant and meet long-term goals. Once a client said to us, "You doing an average job is better than me not doing it at all." Although we will take exception to the "average" part of his comment, we fully appreciate that doing the work is the critical piece.

Ongoing monitoring is critical to long-term success. The beautiful kitchen/bath remodel of ten or fifteen years ago will show its age as time passes. Unfortunately, the shelf life for portfolio design is not even that long. Too often people will use the phrase "buy and hold" as a description for their investing style. From my perspective the term "buy and hold" is an anti-timing statement, not one where any company, mutual fund, or exchange-traded fund (ETF) is "good forever." Things change quickly and often dramatically in today's world. The number of "Top 100" corporations is in a constant state of flux, and portfolios need to accommodate change to continue to have relevance toward meeting objectives.

For the most part, the ongoing process of managing a portfolio is the same as it was to develop the portfolio in the first place. An asset allocation is chosen, and individual investments and managers are selected and implemented. The same criteria used to start are used to continue to assess the portfolio. If an investment or manager no longer fits within the top category, the question needs to be asked if you should keep it at all. There can be reasons, of course! The underperformance may have only been for a short time, and this is common in selecting active managers. I can't tell you how many times we've put a manager on the "watch list," and then saw the manager come back and reward our patience. Yet still, in some cases, change is necessary. Often, a "style drift" takes place. Often, the reason a particular manager is chosen is because he or she has demonstrated a skill in a certain "style." However, managers' investment styles can change over time. Of course, if asked, these managers will have a "reason" for "drifting." Ultimately, the investor needs to ascertain whether or not the new style still fits his or her portfolio. If not, it's probably time to move on. Another reason to move on is a change in the management of the strategy. Most often the reason a particular fund was chosen was the skill of the previous management. A change to another member of the investment management team of the strategy may not be so dramatic as to require an immediate change, but does warrant monitoring. It is very easy to justify keeping an underperforming manager. At the same time, discipline in the process is critical for long-term success.

Benchmarking portfolio investments can be very simple. Pick an index and compare all the strategies and the portfolio to it. For example, you could pick the S&P 500. For those who live in the United States, this is a very popular and widely followed index. Or what about the Dow Jones Industrial Average—also widely known and followed? While over the long run a well diversified portfolio provides high probability results when comparing a diversified portfolio of stocks, bonds, and alternatives and will most of the time look very attractive compared to the Dow

Jones or the S&P 500, and at other times appear to not measure up. Is that comparison really providing the insight you need? Maybe you need a blended benchmark with the S&P 500 and a bond index like the Barclay's US Aggregate Bond. You could roughly construct an index in percentages of equities and fixed income in the mix of the current portfolio. But wait! What if there are international equities? A common approach has been to use the MSCI EAFE index, but if there is an allocation to emerging markets, this will have some failings as well. Then the MSCI All Country World (ACWI) index may be a better comparative tool.

The best tools we find are to compare like indexes with like investment strategies. For example, you could compare an all-cap domestic manager with the Russell 3000 to get a better idea of the total picture of both large and small caps. The S&P 500 would be a reasonable proxy for large-cap stocks.

Even more challenging is measuring the performance of the various alternative strategies. There are a variety of indexes to reference, including some by Credit Suisse that can be found online. Again, by using relevant indexes, you can more accurately assess the performance of the various alternative investment strategies in a portfolio.

You can further put together a blended index on your portfolio using the various indexes in the universe. While fifty thousand indexes is a daunting number, the process can be made more focused by searching for relevant indexes and ignoring the rest.

Earlier I posed the question "Does any of this help investors with diversified portfolios?" A portfolio designed with contemporary design concepts does bring a level of complexity. At the same time, is the investor going down the right path measuring a portfolio on a "relative" basis, relative to what an idea or a market does? Earlier in the book we explored the differences between "relative" and "absolute" returns, with "relative" meaning relatively new, in the last sixty years. The "relative" approach is very relevant in comparing the skill levels of managers and strategies that comprise a piece of the portfolio. After all, we are seeking to be at least average in the case of an index or passive approach. If the tracking error is larger than expected, some action may be appropriate. In the case of active managers, we are seeking the top 20 percent and not the bottom 80 percent; otherwise, we should just index. Relative performance has a role and an important one. Data for these comparisons, which should be done frequently, can be found online or purchased.

But the question "Does this help investors with diversified portfolios?" is still lingering. My view is no, it does not help the individual investor at the level that he or she needs the most. Most investors are seeking to use the portfolio to meet their long-term needs. The über wealthy are excluded from this process because they have such significant wealth that it really doesn't matter what they earn on their portfolios. They can invest at .03 percent interest, and their lives won't really change. Of course, I recognize that they do care; they wouldn't have achieved their wealth if they didn't. With that said, the real challenge for most investors is to invest to offset inflation over time. The essence of a plan is to have capital to meet short- and long-term needs. The biggest obstacle is inflation. Looking at decades of research, we will see in the chart on page 128 from the Federal Reserve that fixed-income investing does not provide the inflation hedge most people need to meet their goals.

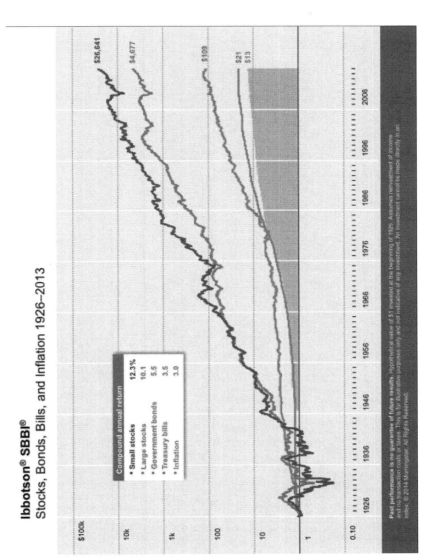

Ibbotson® SBBI®
Stocks, Bonds, Bills, and Inflation 1926–2013

Compound annual return	
• Small stocks	12.3%
• Large stocks	10.1
• Government bonds	5.5
• Treasury bills	3.5
• Inflation	3.0

$26,641
$4,677
$109
$21
$13

1926 1936 1946 1956 1966 1976 1986 1996 2006

@Morningstar 2014 – See Important Notice in Appendix page 162

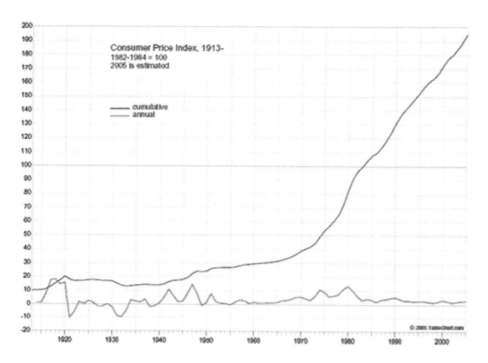

Shouldn't the investment objective being measured be closely aligned with the desired outcome? In the cases of most of the hundreds of clients we have worked with over the past four decades, if one can earn 3, 4, 5, or 6 percent over inflation, the goals can be realized. This proves true for pre- and post-retirees alike. Another benefit is that it provides a more realistic alignment with how the income need is changing. Through the 2000s and early 2010s, the inflation rate was very low. At the same time, both equity and fixed-income returns were lower as well. If the portfolio is still earning over a three- to five-year basis, a reasonable margin over inflation is it not successful? The objective of the individual's life and the goals of that life are paramount, not some frame of what returns used to be. Remembering the double-digit returns of the 1990s does nothing but cause frustration. Making progress toward realizing life's dreams and realizing financial security is a much better place to be.

Living in a manic/depressive frame of mind is a choice when it comes to measuring investment results.

Remember: investing is not the stock market. Investing is allocating resources to meet goals and dreams. The stock market is part of that, but it shouldn't be all of it.

CHAPTER 14

FINDING AND VETTING ADVISORS

Short-term clients look for gurus. Long-term clients want sages. There are no gurus.

—*Harold Evensky*

In my nearly forty years in the financial services business, I've had the opportunity to see a multitude of changes. The financial planning profession really got its start in the late 1960s. Until then you were a stockbroker, life insurance agent, or mutual fund salesperson. Over time since then, the new profession of providing advice separate from product sales evolved and grew. It turns out that change can be very difficult, and the new names that many are using to describe themselves today, such as "financial advisor" and "financial consultant," are the examples of the confusion that exists in the marketplace At the same time, however, the same role—selling financial products—is a key function of what these professionals need to do to make a living. No sale, no money. The choice of a financial advisor based on how objective they will treat their clients is further complicated by the varying levels of compensation an "advisor" will earn based on the products he or she recommends. There are still products in the investment product world that pay exorbitant commissions or finder's fees, sometimes as high as 8 percent upfront. This is an expensive way to invest, but even more onerous are the hidden costs to pay advisors for their "no upfront fee" or "commission-free" product offerings. In reality, the product will often have a nontransparent 12b-1 fee or other percentage of investments that the "advisor" gets paid over a number of years.

> ## Four Horsemen Clues
>
> By now some readers are probably saying, "Got it! I'm ready to go." Others recognize that they have other interests than engaging in this process.
>
> Others will engage a financial advisor for the same reasons people hire personal trainers and coaches. This chapter is dedicated to the latter.

Selecting from a list of products that pay a commission is limiting in and of itself. There are thousands of no-load offerings that can be part of the screening process, providing a broader and deeper pool from which to select. Interestingly, when our firm does cast a wide net such as this, the more expensive, commission-based products never seem to appear. Interesting, isn't it? Cost is a factor. But more important is that our clients deserve to know what the conflicts of interest are in a relationship, and sources of compensation are a relevant and vital piece of information to know.

Unfortunately, too often the questions asked by consumers of financial advice with regard to compensation and costs are obfuscated by industry lingo, with terms such as "fee-based" or "no upfront costs." Let's take on the first one, fee-based. What fee-based really means is that I can and will likely charge you a fee of some type. It *does not mean* that I will not include a product I can also earn a commission on. The conflict of interest comes from the source of the compensation. If it's from a third party, the possibility exists that the person owes some form of allegiance to that third party or may have financial incentive to recommend one solution over another. Let me hasten to add that there are many honest, hardworking, and ethical people who sell products and earn a commission in the financial services business. The key is disclosure.

A term that sounds very much like "fee-based" is the term "fee-only," but in reality they are very, very different in the types of expectations a prospective client may have. A fee-only advisor receives compensation only from clients in the form of fees. Much like an attorney or CPA, the obligation is to serve the client. Since no other compensation will be accepted, there is no conflict in regard to selecting one product versus another. The objective is to provide service to a client and nothing more.

So for most individuals seeking help with their financial strategies, seeking a fee-only advisor simplifies the selection process, because they can concern themselves less with whether an advisor is looking out for their best interests. The fee-only movement is also a fairly new development in the evolution of delivering financial advice. Until recently, only the über wealthy could hire all the advisors they felt necessary. A current trend is for teams of advisors within large financial institutions to remove themselves and become fee-only registered investment advisors independent from the influence of their previous employment relationship. What many people don't fully appreciate is that two regulatory schemes exist in the oversight of the financial advice industry. One is the Financial Industry Regulatory Authority (FINRA), formerly known as the National Association of Securities Dealers (NASD). FINRA is a self-regulating organization that is governed by the broker-dealer community. Within its role is licensing of brokers, and it oversees compliance for both the firms and the individually licensed representatives. The other is the Securities and Exchange Commission (SEC). Unlike FINRA, the SEC is an agency of the US government and oversees the registration of registered investment advisors (RIA) and investment companies such as mutual funds, as well as individual security registrations, quarterly reports for public entities, and broker-dealer entities.

While both regulatory entities oversee the industry of financial advice, they both have differing views when it comes to its oversight. For example, FINRA's guideline as to whether or not investment advice is delivered appropriately is if the investment is "suitable" for the investor. In other words, the broker/advisor needs to know the customer's situation and that the offered product was not inappropriate for the situation.

"Inappropriate" or "suitable" is a very different standard than a fiduciary standard. A fiduciary standard goes further than suitable. Suitable in many ways says it's okay for you. A fiduciary standard basically says, "Based on the trust you have placed in me as your advisor, I will give you the best advice, not just a good choice." There currently exists a debate between the two regulatory authorities regarding bringing the two into harmony. This process of harmonization is a difficult one. On one hand, FINRA maintains that many of its members should not be held to a fiduciary standard, and appropriately so. But in the near term, as a consumer of financial advice, you do deserve to know under what standards an advisor operates and your due diligence in seeking an advisor will need to ask questions about their compensation methodologies and other conflicts of interests.

In the process of seeking advisors, there are places to source advisors, questions to ask, and regulatory sources to validate information. In seeking an advisor, asking friends and relatives for recommendations is a reasonable place to start. They may have had good experiences and be willing to share the names of advisors they have been happy with. Inquiring the same with your family attorney or accountant or tax preparer is often a good choice as well. Care should be exercised in the accounting or tax preparer area, as often there is a financial planning department within the firm, whose staff may not be as objective, because there may be "expectations" from management about cross-referrals in the firm. Or course, that does not mean those professionals would be a bad choice, just that their objectivity may be compromised.

There are also resources in the association arena. You can visit the website of the Financial Planning Association (FPA; fpanet.org) for a listing of financial planners in the area where you live. This will likely include those who operate on a fee-only as well as fee-based basis. The National Association of Professional Financial Advisors (NAPFA; NAPFA.org) is an association of practitioners who operate on a fee-only basis only.

Of course, the identification process is only the beginning. Next would be conducting phone interviews with likely candidates. Questions about how the advisor operates and the types of clients they work with will provide an appropriate initial screening. Then you can select a few to interview in person. Before investing your time in an in-person interview, do a Google search and make sure the individual and the firm are in order. I would be concerned if some negative things come up, but some might be explained away. Better to know first and ask questions than to find out something negative later. Also, check to see if there have been any regulatory issues by using the broker check function at http://www.finra.org/Investors/ToolsCalculators/BrokerCheck/. A check into the firm at sec.gov is also in order. You can learn about the firm's size, disclosures, etc. by reviewing the Form ADV. Some of the information you find may generate some good questions for the in-person interview.

A key function of the in-person interview is to see if you like the person. You will be expected to share a lot of information of a very personal nature. If you are uncomfortable with the person, there is probably a good reason why. Even though it might be that the person is simply having a bad day, in the long run, things often end as they begin. If you are not comfortable with the advisor during the in-person interview, it's probably best to move on. Questions about background, philosophy, and compensation will be key functions of the in-person interview. The appendix presents a questionnaire you can use as a guideline. The other form included in the Appendix, the Fiduciary Oath, can help ferret out those who plan to be fiduciaries and those who don't.

CHAPTER 15

CONCLUSION

*Everything should be made as simple as possible,
but not simpler.*

—*Albert Einstein*

I t is often said that the more things change, the more they stay the same. The first two horsemen of the investor's apocalypse have been adversaries of investors for ages. The new challenges brought by the financial services marketing machine, also known as the third horseman, or the "sea of sameness," brings new and different challenges for investors. The constant and accelerating changes brought about by dislocations and global shifts add additional complexity to successfully meeting long-term goals and dreams.

There are many new realities in the world of investing, but there are also a number that do stay the same. It has always been true that if you invest when an asset is on the higher end of valuations, the longer it will take to achieve the expected returns. It is still true that when you buy low, it is easier to make a profit. Putting all your eggs in one basket has always been a questionable strategy. There are more eggs to choose from today, but broad diversification presents more opportunities than ever before. Investing has always required process and work, and that is certainly true today. The choices are many, but the tools to sift through the many have never been better. The investment industry continues to put new wrappers on old ideas and concepts, but with some effort and common sense, the wrappers can be cast off and a proper evaluation can be made.

Although the quantity of data pieces and information available through the media has never been more numerous, much of it should be ignored. Although many of the investing broadcasts can be entertaining, there are many options for entertainment, such as Turner Classic Movies or the Syfy channel. When it comes to investing, the offerings of these channels will likely be as helpful. Investors need to shut out the "noise" of the markets and focus on long-term strategies with a keen eye toward relative value, recognizing that in reality there are things we do know, but what we don't know is significant, and focusing on asymmetrical risk is a valuable and profitable endeavor. It's best to focus on proven techniques and not the latest and greatest investment scheme. Remember that there's a significant difference from a marketing person selling investment products and advisors who look out for your best interests. With a detailed process and due diligence, the difference can become obvious.

The need to sort, sift, and filter information has never been greater. Nothing worthwhile is accomplished without work and intelligent processes. Business demands, family, and what can seem like constant communication can easily distract us from our goal of establishing financial security for ourselves and our loved ones. Without a doubt, the four horsemen of inflation, volatility, group think/sea of sameness, and global displacements and transformations will do their best to wage war on investors' portfolios. The successful path to fending off the four horsemen of the investor's apocalypse is paved with process, work, and ongoing diligent effort. Whether you are traveling alone or with a trusted advisor, you can navigate that path safely and effectively.

APPENDIX

The forms in this appendix are intended to provide the reader with tools to gather information and may be used as a starting point for the reader's personal tool development.

Fiduciary Oath

The advisor shall exercise his/her best efforts to act in good faith and in the best interests of the client. The advisor shall provide written disclosure to the client prior to the engagement of the advisor, and thereafter throughout the term of the engagement, of any conflicts of interest, which will or reasonably may compromise the impartiality or independence of the advisor. The advisor, or any party in which the advisor has a financial interest, does not receive any compensation or other remuneration that is contingent on any client's purchase or sale of a financial product. The advisor does not receive a fee or other compensation from another party based on the referral of a client or the client's business.

REQUEST FOR PROPOSAL

*** 2014

PART I

PURPOSE, MINIMUM REQUIREMENTS, AND SCOPE OF SERVICES

A. <u>PURPOSE</u>

1. White Oaks Investment Management Inc. is a private invest-ment management firm, with total assets under management of $281 million, located in Long Boat Key, Florida. White Oaks Investment Management Inc. currently manages LLCs to pro-vide more efficient management of its clients' assets at lower costs.

2. This Request for Proposal ("RFP") is issued by White Oaks Investment Management Inc. for the purpose of hiring one investment management firm to provide investment man-agement services for an active _____. The expected total mandate value will be five accounts (one in each LLC) with a total of around _____. The Manager will have full dis-cretion to manage the portfolio consistent with White Oaks Investment Management Investment Policy & Goal Statement

and the terms of the contract between White Oaks Investment Management and the Manager. The Manager's performance objective will be to exceed the return of the _____.

3. Proposals are being solicited from a select group of emerging markets management firms that were screened for appropriateness using White Oaks Investment Management's investment philosophy.

B.   <u>MINIMUM REQUIREMENTS</u>

To be considered as a Manager for the purpose stated above, the Manager must:

1. Be registered as an investment adviser under the Investment Advisers Act of 1940, or provide proof of bank exemption;

2. Have a minimum of five (5) years of investment management experience in emerging markets;

3. Have a minimum of $100 million of equity assets under management in emerging markets;

4. Have a proven and verifiable five-year record of outperforming the _____ Index using returns that fully comply with AIMR performance reporting standards (note: simulated or back-tested results for any or all of this period are not acceptable);

5. Have proof that at least two-thirds (2/3) of the key emerging markets product investment management team (i.e., portfolio managers and analysts) have worked together continuously for at least five years.

C.   <u>SCOPE OF SERVICES</u>

The Manager will be required to provide the following scope of services to White Oaks Investment Management Inc.:

1. Invest allocated funds in conformity with the investment policy and guidelines of White Oaks Investment Management Inc., as defined in the contract established between White Oaks Investment Management Inc. and the firm. Provide discretionary management of the funds under the contract.

2. Provide periodic reports and information relating to the firm's investment strategy and other pertinent information pertaining to the investment of the White Oaks Investment Management Inc.'s funds, as requested by White Oaks Investment Management Inc. Provide monthly reports on portfolio appraisals, performance evaluation and attribution, and trading activities. In addition the Manager should be available to make one conference call per year with White Oaks Investment Management Inc. for the benefit of its clients.

3. Participate in public meetings on a periodic basis to provide information to White Oaks Investment Management Inc. concerning the investment performance of White Oaks Investment Management Inc.'s portfolio and the firm's investment outlook and strategy for White Oaks Investment Management Inc.'s portfolio.

PART II

ADMINISTRATIVE INFORMATION

A.   <u>INSTRUCTIONS FOR SUBMITTING PROPOSALS</u>

1. Managers responding to this RFP must provide answers to the questions posed in Part III of this RFP. All proposals must be complete in every respect and must answer concisely and clearly all questions proposed by the RFP. Late proposals will not be accepted, and will be returned unopened to the Manager.

2. Proposals shall be submitted with a cover letter stating that the <u>firm meets all of the minimum requirements listed in Part I.B of this RFP,</u> and that the firm is able and willing to provide the type and level of services required to fulfill the mandate proposed in this RFP. The cover letter and the offer made by the proposal, and any clarifications to that proposal, shall be signed by an officer of the offering firm or a designated agent empowered to bind the firm in a contract. The cover letter must also identify any sections of the proposal that the firm is identifying as confidential. (See Disclosure of Proposal Content below.)

3. Proposals should follow the order of questions as they are asked in Part III of this RFP. In response to each question asked in Part III, restate the <u>main</u> question (denoted by a number or a letter) in bold font followed by your answers stated in regular font. Responses should be thorough and answer the specific question asked (including the issues addressed in the bullet points following a question).

4. Proposals must be submitted no later than _____

5. A firm must submit one electronic version of the proposal response, including all appendices, and to:

Bob Klosterman
CEO & CIO
White Oaks Investment Management, Inc.

B. <u>REJECTION OF PROPOSALS</u>

1. Firms responding to this RFP must restrict their proposed investment structure to that specified in this RFP. Alternate or substitute structures will be rejected.

2. _____ reserves the right to reject any or all proposals in whole or in part received by this request, due to noncompliance with the requirements of this RFP or for any other reason. White Oaks Investment Management, Inc. will not pay for any information herein requested, nor is it liable for any costs incurred by the submitting Managers.

3. Managers whose proposals do not meet the mandatory requirements will be so notified. After evaluation of the proposals, selection, and approval by White Oaks Investment Management Inc., all Managers will be notified of the successful firm.

4. White Oaks Investment Management Inc. reserves the right to not hire or to defer the hiring of a firm for these management services.

C. <u>DISPOSITION OF PROPOSALS</u> All proposals become the property of White Oaks Investment Management Inc. and will not be returned to the Manager. Late proposals will be returned to the Manager unopened.

D. <u>SIGNATURE OF MANAGER'S AGENT</u> The offer made by the proposal, and any clarifications to that proposal, shall be signed by an officer of the offering firm or a designated agent empowered to bind the firm in a contract.

E. <u>AWARD OF MANDATE</u> White Oaks Investment Management Inc. reserves the right to award this contract not necessarily to the firm with the lowest fee and cost proposal, but to the firm that will provide the best match to the requirements of the RFP. The successful Manager will be determined in accordance with the evaluation criteria defined by White Oaks Investment Management Inc.

F. <u>EVALUATION OF PROPOSALS</u> An Evaluation Committee will meet to evaluate and score the proposals. Upon completion of the Evaluation Committee's evaluation, finalist interviews will be, and office visits <u>may</u> be, conducted with some candidate firms. Determination of whether to conduct interviews and which firms to interview is at the sole discretion of the Evaluation Committee. A determination to execute a contract may be made by the White Oaks Investment Management Inc. Evaluation Committee without an interview, upon recommendation of the Evaluation Committee.

G. <u>EVALUATION CRITERIA</u>   Proposals will be evaluated using the following criteria:

I.	The Firm's Organization and Staff Qualifications	20%
II.	The Firm's Investment Style and Process	20%
III.	The Firm's Relevant Experience and Investment Performance	20%
IV.	The Firm's Resources	10%
V.	The Firm's Fee Proposal	30%

H. <u>INVESTMENT CONTRACT REQUIREMENTS</u>

1. <u>Duration of Contract Term</u>: The term of the contract is expected to be for a period of four years, with annual evaluations.

2. <u>Termination</u>: The contract may be terminated by either of the parties thereto upon written notice delivered to the other party at least thirty days prior to the intended date of termination.

3. <u>Subcontracting</u>: The contractor shall not subcontract any portion of the services to be performed under the contract without the prior written approval of the White Oaks Investment Management Inc.

4. <u>Standard of Care/Indemnification</u>: The contractor holds itself out as an expert in the investment of large trust or investment funds. The contractor represents itself as being possessed of greater knowledge and skill than the average man. Accordingly, the contractor is under a duty to exercise a skill greater than that of an ordinary man and the manner in which the contractor carries out its duties under the contract will be evaluated in light of the contractor's superior skill. The contractor shall wholly indemnify White Oaks Investment Management Inc. against any and all losses, damages, costs, expenses, legal

fees, and liability resulting from investment advice and other services provided under the contract that are not made in accordance with the provisions contained in this contract, investment advice not made in accordance with the law applicable to the funds for which investment advice is rendered, and advice not made in accordance with the standard of care set forth in this paragraph.

PART III

QUESTIONNAIRE

A) Organization/People (max 2 pages)

   2) Describe the ownership of the firm; include all subsidiaries.

   3) Describe the structure of the group that manages the product.

      a) Describe the role of portfolio managers, research analysts, traders, etc.

      b) Who is responsible for investment strategy, asset allocation, portfolio construction, research, security selection, trading, etc.?

      c) Describe the communication links between the groups within the product area, and across product areas.

   3) Over the past five years, has your organization or any of its affiliates or parent, or any officer or principal been involved in any business litigation or regulatory or legal proceedings? If so, provide an explanation and indicate the current status.

4) Describe any significant developments in your organization (changes in ownership, personnel, business, etc.) over the past five years. Is your firm considering any changes in ownership, business combinations, or other significant organizational changes?

5) Describe the compensation and incentive program for professionals directly involved in the product.

   a) How are they evaluated and rewarded? What incentives are provided to attract and retain superior individuals?

   b) Do you offer direct ownership, phantom stock, profit sharing, and/or performance bonuses?

      (i) Who is eligible to participate?

      (ii) On what basis are these incentives determined—is compensation tied to success factors such as asset growth, performance, or other factors? Please list and indicate the weight of each in determining total compensation.

   c) How does your compensation structure/levels compare with other firms in the industry?

6) Describe the background of the professionals directly involved in the product.

   a) Are they brought in from the outside or promoted to their positions from within the organization?

   b) Is their prior experience in portfolio management/research/trading, industry, consulting, or other business or technical areas?

c) What sort of ongoing education programs (for example, the CFA program) are encouraged or required?

7) Discuss the causes and impact of any turnover (departures or hiring/promotions) of any professionals directly involved in the product you have experienced in the past five years. How long has the team been together?

8) Describe the objectives of your firm with respect to future growth in the product, commenting on:

a) Additional resources for portfolio management, research, trading, client service, and tools/models to enhance the investment process or manage growth.

b) Size limitations with respect to assets under management in the product. How did you arrive at those asset limits? Are companion retail mutual fund assets and assets in this category from broader mandates included in these limits?

B) Philosophy/Process (max 3 pages)

    3) Describe your firm's investment philosophy for the product.

        d) What market anomaly or inefficiency are you trying to capture?

        e) Why do you believe this philosophy will be successful in the future? Provide any evidence or research that supports this belief.

        f) How has this philosophy changed over time?

    2) What percent of resources and time does your firm devote to the top-down aspect of your approach versus the bottom-up (security selection) aspect?

    3) Describe your portfolio construction process.

        a) Are you seeking unique sources of information?

        b) Are you applying unique methods to process the information?

        c) What is the universe from which securities are selected?

        d) What types of securities are used?

        e) How many issues are typically contained in a portfolio?

        f) How are individual security weightings determined?

        g) What latitude is given to individual portfolio managers within the product team? Who has ultimate decision-making authority and accountability?

        h) How is country allocation decided?

4) Describe your buy disciplines.

   e) What valuation approaches are used in evaluating stocks?

   f) What specific fundamental factors (P/B, earnings growth, P/CF, ROE, etc.) are integral to the stock selection process? What is the relative importance of these factors?

   g) What market capitalization and liquidity criteria meet the requirements of your buy discipline?

5) What is the target or expected tracking error and how important is the benchmark tracking error in the portfolio construction process?

   f) Is it measured and managed? If so, how?

   g) Describe your sell disciplines.

      a) What market capitalization and liquidity criteria meet the requirements of your sell discipline?

      b) What factors dictate your sell decision?

      c) Describe what percentage of your sells is driven by position trims versus swaps for more attractive issues versus fundamental deterioration versus mistakes over the course of a year?

      d) Under what circumstances would your firm deviate from these disciplines? Have you ever deviated? If so, please describe.

      e) What has the annual turnover been for this product in each of the last five years?

6) How is portfolio risk managed and monitored? Describe how you monitor and manage:

   a) Residual risk versus the benchmark

   b) Common factor risks

   c) Security, sector, country, and industry weightings

7) Describe any risk measurement models used and how these analyses are incorporated in the portfolio management process.

8) Do you use cash as a method of risk control? Please provide a table that shows the quarterly cash holdings for the subject product in each of the last three years.

9) How do you monitor the product's adherence to its investment style and process? Specify who is responsible.

C) Resources (max 2 pages)

4) If you have internal research capability that is dedicated to the product, describe the research process.

   e) What specific research is conducted?

   f) What are the outputs of the internal research effort?

   g) What percentage of the research effort is conducted internally?

2) If you use external research in the management of the product, describe the external research.

   c) What are the sources of external research?

   d) What specific research is acquired from external sources?

   e) How is this information incorporated in the stock selection and portfolio construction process?

3) Describe the quantitative models and tools you utilize for research, portfolio construction, and trading. What enhancements are being contemplated?

4) If you have a trading function that is exclusive for the product, describe the trading capabilities for the product.

   a) How many dedicated traders are there, and what is their experience?

   b) Describe the trading systems and strategies you use, and indicate any enhancements your firm is contemplating.

   c) Describe how you measure trading costs (commissions and market impact).

d) Provide the annual total transaction costs (commissions and market impact) for the subject product for each of the last five years.

5) Describe how you use soft dollars. List the three largest recipients of soft dollar trades and indicate what percentage they comprise of the overall trading volume generated by the subject product for each of the last three years.

6) What resource constraints exist? What is the basis for obtaining additional resources to support each function for this particular product?

D) Performance (max 3 pages)

5) Provide annual performance results for years ended 12/31, gross of fees, for your firm's discretionary emerging markets composite for each of the last ten years, or since inception, compared to the annual results for the MSCI Emerging Markets Index. Additionally, include performance results for the most recent quarter ended _____.

6) Provide cumulative annualized performance results for periods ended 12/31, gross of fees, for your firm's discretionary composite for three years, five years, seven years, and ten years, compared to the MSCI Emerging Markets Index, as well as the most recent quarter ended [_____].

7) Provide an explanation for individual years where performance is meaningfully different (>100 bps) from the benchmark, either positive or negative.

8) Provide the annual high and low returns within your firm's discretionary composite presented in IV.A above for each annual period ended 12/31 over the last ten years. Describe the causes of meaningful (i.e., >30 bps) return differences. How much is attributable to individual portfolio managers' decisions versus individual client cash flows? Do the same for the most recent period ending _____}.

9) What is the most appropriate expected excess return for your product over a market cycle (i.e., three to five years)? How is this determined?

10) Describe how you analyze and evaluate the performance of the product.

11) Describe how you conduct performance attribution analysis, indicating any models or tools used.

    a) How do you incorporate the results of the performance attribution analysis in the management of the product?

    b) Provide a table that shows performance attribution (i.e., contribution from stock selection, sector allocation, timing, other, etc.) for this product for each of the last five years.

E) Fees (max 1/2 page)

6) Describe how fees are determined for this product. Are fees a function of the expected alpha of the strategy?

7) Describe any performance fee structures you have in place. If you do not, would you be willing to incorporate a performance fee?

8) State your proposed fee for this mandate.

APPENDIX

I. Organizational Chart: Product Structure & Key Professionals

Provide an organizational chart that diagrams the different functions (research, trading, etc.) dedicated to the product area. Professionals should be identified over their areas of responsibility. Indicate the number of years each individual has been in his or her current function.

II. Key Professionals

III. Responsibilities

IV. Turnover

Indicate when and why any professional dedicated to the product (i.e., portfolio managers, analysts, and traders) left or joined the firm in the past five years. What were/are their job responsibilities? For personnel who have left, indicate job titles and years with the firm and who replaced them.

V. ASSETS UNDER MANAGEMENT. Please provide the following information in the prescribed format presented below:

Timeframe	Firm's Total Assets
Most Recent Quarter	
Last Year	
2 years ago	
3 years ago	
4 years ago	
5 years ago	

Asset Class Assumptions Used in Prospective Risk Return Charts

		Annualized Mean	Ann. Standard Deviation
Domestic Equities		8.0%	16.0%
Int'l Dev Equities		9.5%	17.0%
Emerging Mkt Equities		11.0%	24.0%
Bonds		1.0%	3.0%
Cash		0.1%	0.1%
Commodities		5.0%	12.0%
Structured Note		7.0%	13.0%
Material Stocks		8.0%	20.%
MLPs		15.0%	16.0%
Multi Strat Hedge		15.0%	10.0%
Managed Futures		5.0%	12.0%
Equity Long/Short		13.0%	9.0%
Real Estate Loans		9.0%	2.0%
Real Estate Equity		12.0%	5.0%

Assumptions are developed from a variety of sources of historical data. The models are created to illustrate certain concepts at a particular point in time and vary with current circumstances. There is no intention that the assumptions will be or should be used by the reader without their own diligence and assumptions and modifications.

Morningstar Copyright Notice

Made in the USA
San Bernardino, CA
13 January 2015